HOMEMADE CAT FOOD

BALANCED, VET APPROVED RAW FOOD FOR YOUR CAT(A RAW FEEDING GUIDE FOR CATS)

HARSHITA SHIVANAGOWDA

Made with ❤ on the Notion Press Platform
www.notionpress.com

To Lulu Monkiss, for teaching me so much in ten and a half years.
Even nine lifetimes with you won't be enough;
Rest in Peace, my sweet kitty.

Contents

Contents

Foreword

Your Cat is a Carnivore. This means that your cat was built by Mother Nature to get her nutritional needs met by the consumption of other animals, derives very little nutritional benefit from plant-based sources, and ideally should have minimal or no grains in her diet. In her natural environment, your cat would be eating a high-protein, moderate-fat diet with only about four to nine percent of her diet consisting of carbohydrates. Dry foods(kibble) contain somewhere around 35-50 percent carbohydrates. This is not what Mother Nature intended for our carnivore friends.

- ANNE JABLONSKI

Preface

Do you get all fired up about your cats? Are you determined to give them the best in life you can? Then this book is for you!

Cats are extraordinary, fascinating creatures. Sadly, our understanding of our delightful feline companions lags far behind that of their canine counterparts. I'm out to change that, and I'm going to do it by helping you be the best cat owner you can be!

Vets and cat owners are defering to the pet food industry on vital health issues. That's a problem.

Those of us who care about healthy nutrition for cats face confusion and obstacles. Many busy veterinary professionals are permitting the pet food industry to act as their proxy when it comes to nutritional counsel for their clients. The results can be disastrous for cats. I'd love for some of my layperson insights into treating one terrible malady and the lessons I've learned along the way about feline nutrition to be instructive to the veterinary community. And to people like me who were desperate for answers.

What My Cats Taught Me About Nutrition for Cats

My experience with my cats opened my eyes in a big way to how many well-meaning, overworked, and overwhelmed vets are often overlooking the most obvious answer when it comes to dealing with feline illness, especially—but certainly not exclusively—digestive problems.

I am not a vet. I don't presume to know more about feline anatomy than someone who has graduated from veterinary school. I don't treat scores of animals every day or perform all manner of delicate surgeries and lifesaving procedures. My sole 'credential' is that I have spent as lot of time reading about this and I have seen results with my own cats.

The impact that a proper diet can have on a cat seems most conspicuous and immediate for a cat suffering from digestive problems like IBD. But I learned along the way that all kinds of serious feline health disorders can be reversed or improved if we feed these magnificent creatures properly, by sticking as close to Mother Nature as we can manage. Just for starters, that means not feeding dry food to cats.

Some relationships are simply never meant to be. Cats with dry cat food, for instance. I'm here to help you with this break-up. It's an important step to a long and happy life with your cat.

Acknowledgements

Special thanks to Dr Karen Becker, Dr Lisa A. Pierson & Anne Jablonski.

We stand on the shoulders of giants. See the 'Resources & Sources' section for the complete list of integrative veterinarians, feline nutritionists and holistic practictioners whose work has been the foundational in the creation of this book.

Prologue

Diet is the Brick and Mortar of Health: What You Feed Your Cat Matters

Putting a little thought into your decision on what you put inside your furry friend can pay very big dividends over her lifetime and very possibly help her avoid serious, painful and costly illnesses such as kidney disease, bladder stones, cystitis, diabetes, obesity, inflammatory bowel disease, and fatty liver disease.

Learn How to Read a Pet Food Ingredient Label

Not all cat foods are created equal and not all proteins are created equal. Always keep in mind that your cat is a carnivore! This means she has a better shot at good health by consuming animal-based proteins (meat) instead of plant-based proteins (grains). Remember that quality meat is the best first ingredient in a food and that grains supply a less bioavailable form of protein for your cat.

Don't just look at the front label on cat food–look at the ingredient list supplied by the manufacturer. A food that lists grain – like corn, corn gluten meal, or rice as a first ingredient is concerning. The main ingredient in a carnivore's diet SHOULDN'T be grain.

Look for ***real meat*** as the first ingredient, but also pay attention to all the carbohydrate/grain sources in the food. Bear in mind that pet food labels can be deceptive. Ingredients are listed in order of weight, and so manufacturers often split up all of the individual carbohydrate components so that each grain is a lesser weight than the meat product. But if you add up all the grain products in many dry foods, you are left with a large number of grain-based carbohydrates relative to the small amount of actual meat in the food.

Dry Food Is Convenient But It's Not Ideal for a Carnivore.

Water is absolutely vital to your cat's health. Cats on a dry food diet are often chronically dehydrated. This can lead to many health problems. The natural prey of a wild cat contains between 65-75% water. Dry food averages 10% and canned food averages 78% -you can see that a canned diet is much better for meeting your cat's water needs than dry food. Since cats do not have a strong thirst drive compared to other mammals, it is critical that they get plenty of moisture with their food.

Do not be confused by the listing of the protein percentages on dry food compared to canned. At first glance, it would appear that the dry food has a higher amount of protein than the canned food - but this is not true on a dry matter basis which is the accurate way to compare the two foods. Most canned foods, when figured on a dry matter basis, have more protein than the dry food. And remember, the percentage numbers do not tell the whole story. The majority of protein in the canned food is meat-based. The majority of the protein in the dry food is plant-based and is therefore less bioavailable to your cat.

At a bare minimum, use as little dry food as possible, and try to feed a quality canned diet that contains meat – preferably human-grade – as its first ingredient. The resources section has a few good brands I found and use for my own requirements for my cats.

If You Want to Prepare a Homemade Diet – Good for You – But Do it Right.

A home-prepared diet can be the absolute best thing you do for your cat. It can also be the worst. If you're willing to follow a tested and balanced recipe, I can point you toward some good information on selecting ingredients and preparing the food. If your cat is a kibble eating kitty, make sure to transition him/her gradually. Kibble fed kitties have stomach acid that is too high for raw food and suddenly changing the diet might give him/her a stomach upset. Kittens are more amenable to eating their species appropriate diet than their older counterparts, but that doesn't mean you shouldn't try. My kibble fed for 7 years cat, Tubby is taking to raw food really well(with some initial hiccups). If my picky eater can do it, so can yours! For kittens you have to start with ground or finely chopped meat, adult cats can manage chunks or cut pieces. A good pair ot kitchen shears and a cleaver knife are good investments.

Nature knows what a cat should eat. So should you. Switching a cat to a home-prepared diet will take patience. It's usually best to make the transition to a new diet slowly, adding small amounts of the new food to the food they're accustomed to and then gradually changing the ratio. This is particularly true with older cats or cats with extremely sensitive digestive systems. You may have to bribe the cat by adding a familiar flavor to the new food. Cats that are accustomed to an all-dry diet can be very stubborn. A few tricks include: grinding up the dry food into a powder and sprinkling it on the new food; adding in a very amount of juice from a can of tuna; or adding something flavorful like crumbled dehydrated/freeze-dried/frozen/air-dried meat treats to the top of the new raw food to increase her interest.

Kittens are very open to trying raw food.

CHAPTER ONE

A Study In Nutrition in Cats By Dr. Francis M. Pottenger JR, MD

From 1932 to 1942, Dr. Francis Marion Pottenger, Jr. conducted an experiment to determine the effects of heat-processed food on cats. This ten-year cat study was prompted by the high death rate among his laboratory cats undergoing operations to remove their adrenal glands. I have to admit I don't like the reason he was doing the study, because it involved adrenalectomies (surgical removal of the adrenal glands) of cats for use in standardizing the hormone content of the adrenal extract he was making for a possible cure for Tuberculosis. At that time, there were no chemical procedures to measure the strength of adrenal extract. So, manufacturers used cats. Cats die without their adrenal glands. So, the amount of extract the cats needed to keep them alive allowed the manufacturers to calibrate the strength of their product.

Concerned with the cats poor postoperative survival, Dr. Pottenger noticed the cats showed a decrease in their reproductive capacity and many of the kittens born in the laboratory had skeletal deformities and organ malfunctions. By a quirk of fate, since the number of cats donated by his neighbors in Monrovia, California kept increasing, he couldn't handle the demand for cooked meat scraps. So, he ordered raw meat scraps from a local meat packing plant, including the viscera, muscle and bone. Always a scientist, Dr. Pottenger fed these raw meat scraps to a segregated group of cats so that he could observe any change; within a few months, this raw fed group appeared healthier, their kittens more vigorous, and they had a higher survival rate after their operations.

The Experiment

Pottenger conceived of an experiment in which one group of cats received only raw milk and raw meat, while other groups received part of the diet as pasteurized milk or cooked meat. He found that only those cats whose diet was completely raw survived the surgical procedure he performed, and as his research progressed, he noticed that only the all-raw group continued in good health generation after generation. They had excellent bone structure, freedom from parasites and vermin, easy pregnancies and gentle dispositions. Dr. Pottenger fed his cats a diet of raw and pasterised milk milk, cod liver oil, cooked meat scraps(liver, tripe, sweetbreads, brains, heart and muscle) and raw meat scraps.

All of the groups whose diet contained even partially cooked meat developed "facial deformities" of the exact same kind that Price observed in human groups on the "displacing foods of modern commerce" – narrowed faces, crowded jaws, frail bones and weakened ligaments. They were plagued with parasites, developed all manner of diseases and had difficult pregnancies. Female cats became aggressive while the males became docile. After just three generations, young animals died before reaching adulthood and reproduction ceased.

The contrast between the two sets of cats was so startling; it prompted Dr. Pottenger to perform a controlled experiment to verify these facts scientifically. The experiment included 900 cats over four generations and was well documented by Dr. Pottenger in his book. The cats were divided into five groups. All the groups were supplied the same basic minimal diet, but the major portion of the diets was varied. Two of the groups were fed whole foods (raw milk and meat - real foods for cats). The other three groups were given processed foods: pasteurized, evaporated and condensed milk.

All four generations of the raw meat and raw milk groups remained healthy throughout their normal lifespan. The first generation of all three processed food groups developed diseases and illnesses near the end of their lives. The second generation of all three processed food groups developed diseases and illnesses in the middle of their lives. The third generation of all three processed food groups developed diseases and illnesses in the beginning of their lives and many died before six months of age. There was no fourth generation in any of the three processed food groups. Either the third generation parents were sterile or the fourth generation cats were died before birth! It was found that all four generations of the raw food groups were healthy throughout their normal lifespan.

What makes the Pottenger's Study groundbreaking is that it was conducted over generations of cats, not just over weeks or months, but over years. In a sharp contrast to this method, most studies today last for a short duration, most animals are euthanised later and if they aren't euthanised, there is usually no follow up.

The Conclusion for cats– and humans?

Dr. Francis Pottenger, like his counterpart Dr. Weston A. Price, was a researcher. His studies revealed that predictable changes in health can occur when you change the diet. In his study, cats that were fed a diet of raw meat, raw milk and cod liver oil lived generation after generation in good health. When the raw food was replaced by pasteurized milk and partially cooked meat, allergies and skeletal deformities occurred in the first generation. The offspring of these poorly fed cats developed glandular problems – thyroid, adrenal and pancreatic. The next generation experienced a whole host of degenerative diseases, and the fourth generation exhibited mental disorders and was infertile, meaning they did not reproduce. The implication for humans? The human diet produces "facial deformities," as we are seeing these days and as documented by the work of Dr Weston A Price; extinction will occur if that diet is followed for several generations.

As for as applying his results to human nutrition, Dr. Pottenger said, "While no attempt will be made to correlate the changes in the animals studied with malformations found in humans, the similarity is so obvious that parallel pictures will suggest themselves." There is no similar experiment in medical literature. The findings were supervised by Dr. Pottenger along with Dr. Alvin Foord, professor of pathology at the University of Southern California and pathologist at the Huntington Memorial Hospital in Pasadena. These studies met the most rigorous scientific standards of their day.

The Pottenger's Study should not be misinterpreted to mean that humans should eat only raw foods – humans are not cats. In fact the human optimal diet is more similar to the optimal canine diet, than an optimal feline diet(humans and dogs are omnivores, cats are carnivores). Part of the diet was cooked in all the healthy groups Price studied. Milk products, however, were almost always consumed raw.

Pottenger's findings must be seen in the context of the Price research and can be interpreted as follows: When the human diet produces facial deformities – the progressive narrowing of the face and crowding of the teeth – extinction will occur if that diet is followed for several generations. The implications for western civilization – obsessed as it is with refined, highly sweetened, mostly cooked convenience foods and low-fat items – is profound.

For more information, Read the book Pottenger's Cats - A Study In Nutrition by Dr. Francis J Pottenger Jr.

CHAPTER TWO

The Problem With Commercial Dry Cat Food

This chapter lays out some often-ignored principles of feline nutrition and explains why cats have a better chance at optimal health if they are fed wet/canned/frozen raw food (or a balanced homemade diet) instead of dry kibble. Most people don't even know that there are many more options apart from the generic vet store Wet & Dry food we see on pet food aisles.

Let's get our terminology right:
Whenever I say Kibble in the book, it refers to Cat Dry Food. Wet food generally means Cat Food in pouches or cans(also called Canned Food). While Wet Food is one step better than Kibble, keeping meat and meat by products stable at room temperatures requires a lot of artificial preservatives. Supplements are also added to counter this nutritional degradation. Wet food is made from non-human grade meat, has a lot of fillers and is usually heat processed so it is not really raw and species-appropriate.When I say

'canned food' in some cases, it refers to human-grade canned food and not necessarily commericial wet cat food.

The other cat food options most cat owners aren't aware of are:

1. Canned human-grade meats(like Tuna, Sardines, anchovy in water or oil)
2. Dehydrated Raw Meats,
3. Freeze dried or Air Dried Raw Meat
4. Frozen Raw Food

Putting a little thought into what you feed your cat(s) can pay big dividends over their lifetime and very possibly help them avoid serious, painful, and costly illnesses. An small but increasing number of nutrition-savvy veterinarians, including board-certified veterinary internists, are now strongly recommending the feeding of canned food instead of dry kibble.

The three key negative issues associated with Kibble are:

1) water content is too low
2) carbohydrate is too high
3) type of protein – too high in processed plant-based versus animal-based proteins

In addition, dry food is very heavily processed which includes being subjected to high temperatures for a long time resulting in alteration and destruction of nutrients. Dry food is also often contaminated with bacteria, fungal mycotoxins, storage mites/cockroaches and their feces, etc. Most people who are concerned about their own nutrition have heard nutritionists say "shop the perimeter of the grocery store." This statement refers to the push to get humans to focus on fresh whole food – not overly processed food found in boxes and cans. Where do you think kibble would reside in this scenario? Definitely not in the "perimeter"! There is nothing fresh about this source of food and it certainly does not come close to resembling a bird or a mouse.

Also keep in mind that dry foods are not refrigerated and they sit in warm warehouses, on pet store shelves, and in your cupboards for weeks or months before your pets consume them. Fats can easily become rancid, and bacteria will proliferate, in this type of environment. There is no doubt that dry food is responsible for far more health problems, and other diseases, than most veterinarians and cat owners realize.

Many of us feed cats as per our convenience. But, cats are obligate carnivores and need to be fed real meat (and other animal parts).

Nutrition is the building block upon which every living creature's health is built, and this applies doubly so to obligate carnivores whose dietary needs are so sharply defined. Like birds of prey, snakes and sharks, praying mantis and dragonflies, cats are designed inside and out to catch and eat whole prey. Every aspect of feline physiology demonstrates that obtaining what a cat needs to achieve optimum health — not just survive but truly thrive — depends fulfilling its fresh prey-based dietary requirements,

Raw Diet Benefits

- Improved digestion
- Increased energy
- Better urinary tract and kidney health
- Better oral health
- Optimal condition and weight
- Healthy coat, Less shedding, Fewer/No hairballs
- Greatly reduced stool odor and volume

Cats have no dietary need for carbohydrates.
Since the cat's natural diet contains negligible amounts Of carbohydrates, cats process carbs ineffectively and lack some of the enzymatic pathways needed to convert them into energy. Without pathways for energy conversion, carbs are turned into glucose and stored as fat. Digesting carbs stresses the cat's digestive system, causing inflammation and reducing protein absorption. Feline satiety is signaled by animal protein: without sufficient amounts of it, cats will consistently overeat. Excess carbs in the diet, especially grains, leads to obesity, diabetes and serious digestive problems such as IBD, kidney issues and intestinal cancer.

Obligate carnivores metabolize animal protein and fat for energy.
Cats are metabolically adapted for preferential use of animal protein and fat as energy sources and animal tissues effectively and thoroughly, obtaining maximal nutrition with minimal effort. They have a hard-wired requirement for animal protein to fuel basic bodily functions and if the diet does not contain enough, they will sabotage the muscles in their own bodes to get what they need to meet that requirement.

Cats need a high water content in their food.
Cats evolved as desert creatures that had their water needs met through their prey, and they have a comparatvely low thirst drive and are unable to drink enough water to meet their 62% dietary requirement. Cats fed primarily dry kibble are chronically dehydrated and at risk for developing urinary and kidney problems (among other issues).

Feed your cat a biologically appropriate, natural diet.
This is the only diet that fits your cat's true nutritional requirements, Even cats fed premium canned products/

exhibit unmistakable signs of improved vitality and health when transitioned to a balanced raw diet. Raw might involve a bit more time and planning., but your cat will have a healthier, happier. and longer life – well worth the extra effort.

Why No Kibble!

Kibble is likely the single largest underlying cause of most of the diseases and other illnesses sweeping in epidemic proportions across our domestic cat populations. Obesity, diabetes, urinary tract issues, inflammatory bowel disease (often a precursor for intestinal cancer, or lymphoma), kidney disease, skin and ear allergies, vomiting and diarrhea are just a few of the ailments that have been traced back to kibble diets. Our beloved cats – like birds of prey, sharks and snakes – have exceptionally specialized gastrointestinal systems built to process a very specific diet of animal parts, not highly-processed, synthetically supplemented dry cereal bits. Put the wrong type of fuel in a high-performance engine long enough and you will ruin that engine.

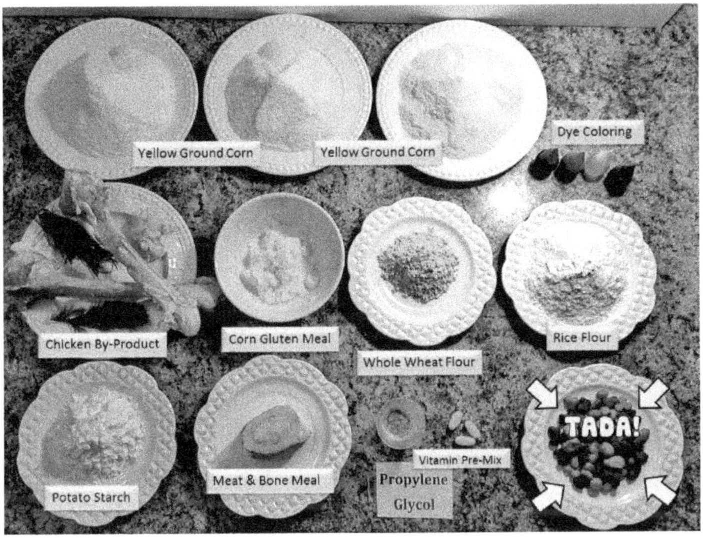

Rodney Habib, of Planet Paws Pet Essentials, created this infographic in his own kitchen to help pet food consumers understand what really goes into the creation of kibble products.

I've added this photo here so you can take a close look at these ingredients. Ground corn (lots of it), toxic dyes, bones, beaks and feathers, more corn, wheat and rice flour, potato starch, unidentified meat and bone meal, Propylene Glycol (defined by dictionary.com as a colorless, viscous, hygroscopic liquid; used chiefly as a lubricant, as an antifreeze, as a heat transfer fluid, and as a solvent), and a vitamin premix almost guaranteed to be sourced from China. This wouldn't even be a healthy diet for you and me to eat, and we're omnivores built to digest a wide variety of nutrient sources. Think about that for a minute.

Now just imagine how profoundly unhealthy this has to be for a carnivore whose digestive physiology is uniquely, beautifully designed for one thing – the exclusive consumption of other animal meats, bones and organs. Imagine how these pets feel, living on a diet their bodies aren't meant to process, day in and day out, year after year. Tired, perpetually hungry, achy and grumpy probably doesn't even begin to describe it.

And, of course, pet food ingredients are not the pretty fresh products you see in this picture, but are, instead, the garbage and leftovers from the human food and agricultural industries. This explains why nearly 100% of the top ten most common canine and feline diseases, as recorded by Veterinarian Pet Insurance (VPI) since 2004, have links to poor nutrition, doesn't it?

Transition Tips

First step: If you are free-feeding, you need to switch to scheduled meals, three a day (four for kittens). This is important for a variety of reasons, over and above the fact a free-fed cat will have no incentive to eat anything new you offer.

Obesity is probably the most important of those reasons you have start transitioning NOW! The cat's sense of satiety is triggered by the presence of a certain amount of animal-based protein in her meal. If there is not enough of that protein, or if it is in a form the cat's body does not recognize (as happens when those proteins are altered by the extremely high temperatures of kibble processing), the cat will keep returning to the bowl as long as food is present. Since carbs are converted almost directly into fat, and the vast majority of kibble products are very high carb, this almost invariably leads to obesity. Kibble-fed cats are perpetually hungry. Obesity, besides being very uncomfortable to an animal that evolved for an athletic life of running, leaping and climbing, the cat's ability to groom will eventually become affected, causing dirty fur, itchy skin and general unhappiness. Obese cats are also at risk for diabetes.

In addition, a carnivore's digestive physiology has incorporated hunger as an integral part of its healthy workings. Indigestible solids are retained in the stomach until digestion of other food products is completed and it is, in fact, hunger pangs which propel this material forth. If the cat is never allowed to become hungry, that movement is compromised, leading to discomfort, hairball regurgitation and other digestive issues.

Lisa Pierson from CatInfo.org has written a great deal about transitioning cats off kibble. If you are switching from kibble to raw, or even kibble to canned to raw, you can also join CatCentric's Facebook group to ask questions and get help.

On September 22, 2011, the Winn Feline Foundation highlighted a study that, among other things, linked kibble diets to urinary tract blockages (Feline Urethral Obstruction). During a panel at the 2010 Institute of Food Technologists (IFT) Annual Meeting and Food Expo, Dr. Demian Dressler, a highly-regarded veterinarian oncologist, talked about his research conclusively linking kibble to cancer, and decried the pet food industry's practices of using ingredients detrimental to the health of the pets for whom their products are intended.

Top 10 Pet Medical Conditions of 2011 (Source: VPI Pet Insurance)

1. Bladder Infection
2. Chronic Kidney Disease

3. Overactive Thyroid
4. Upset Stomach
5. Periodontitis/Dental Disease
6. Diabetes
7. Intestinal Upset/Diarrhea
8. Ear Infection
9. Skin Allergies
10. Lymphosarcoma (Cancer of Lymph Node)

Top 10 Pet Medical Conditions of 2010 (Source: VPI Pet Insurance)

1. Lower Urinary Tract Disease
2. Gastritis/Vomiting
3. Chronic Renal Failure
4. Hyperthyroidism
5. Diabetes
6. Enteritis/Diarrhea
7. Skin Allergy
8. Periodontitis/Dental Disease
9. Ear Infection
10. Upper Respiratory Infection

Notice how the No.1 medical condition pets are rushed to the emergency veterinary clinic is Bladder Infection and Lower UTI disease.

Kibble has a Shelf Life

If you choose to use kibble, please know it does have an expiration date. Plus, without a few basic food safety precautions that expiration date may not be viable, potentially leading to a range of health issues.

Dry food or kibble is made by combining ingredients into a slurry, processed through an extruder under pressure, and then heated to dry. To make the formed pellets palatable, even irresistible, once dried, the food is sprayed with animal fats and digest. What's often not discussed is the susceptibility of this highly processed food to handling and storage conditions.

Earlier dry foods used chemical preservatives, but when these preservatives were found to be health risks, many pet food manufacturers moved to natural preservatives. Although considered safer for our pets, these pet foods can be more fragile and at greater risk of spoilage.

When purchasing, make sure there are no holes or tears in the bag and there is a generous expiration date. Because once opened, the expiration countdown accelerates. Buy only what you need for a month. A way to prolong freshness is to set aside what you may need for a week or so, then freeze the remaining. Use freezer-safe containers and make sure to wash the containers with hot water and detergent before reusing.

Freezing also helps prevent storage mite contamination, which is a common allergen in cats and dogs.

Storage mites are frequently found in cat and dog foods especially once the bag is opened.

If using a pet food container/bin, leave the food in the original bag and place inside the container. Or be sure to wash between uses. This prevents the fats from lingering in the container and deteriorating, as well as reducing the risk of mold.

Be sure to store foods in a cool, dry location, away from heating vents, sun exposure, and strong-smelling cleaners or scents.

Don't trust your nose for freshness. The noses of cats and dogs are far superior to yours. If your pet has been eating its food and then turns away, (s)he may be telling you something. Years before I was researching the pet food industry and animal nutrition, our dog turned away from a new bag of food. Even with tempting toppers, he flat out refused. That food ended up being in one of the biggest pet food recalls in history for mycotoxins(naturally occurring toxins produced by molds that cause serious health effects to humans and animals).

And finally, do not soak your pet's dry food unless your pet eats it immediately. Naturally occurring molds can be found in pet food ingredients including grains and pulses. When kibble is soaked in water or broth, then left out for an extended period of time, that moisture creates the perfect environment for bacteria to flourish, turning their food into a petri dish.

From The Experts

Much has been written about this subject by highly-educated veterinarians, feline nutritionists and other experts. Below are a few quotes from some of those experts, as well as links to their articles or sites.

For further information on the health implications of feeding kibble, see CatInfo.org by Dr. Pierson and the Feline Nutrition Education Society's site. For examples of amazing improvements in health and vitality, check out the testimonials on FelineInstincts.

Dr. Lisa Pierson, Feeding Your Cat: Know The Basics of Feline Nutrition

"Cats have a physiological decrease in the ability to utilize carbohydrates due to the lack of specific enzymatic pathways that are present in other mammals, and the lack a salivary enzyme called amylase. Cats have no dietary need for carbohydrates and, more worrisome is the fact that a diet that is high in carbohydrates can be detrimental to their health..."

Dr. Elizabeth Hodgkins, Diabetes and Obesity: Preventable Epidemics

"If you worry about switching forms of food because you

have been convinced that dry food is essential to good dental health for your cat, consider this: veterinarians today, whose feline patients are almost always consuming dry food as their complete or nearly complete diet, are seeing as much oral and dental disease in their patients as ever before. While the feeding of a crunchy kibble may have an intuitive appeal for dental health, the reality is that there are no scientific studies that prove dry foods provide better dental health throughout a cat's life than wet foods do. In my practice, I have a majority of my patients consuming exclusively wet diets. My patients require no more regular dental care and experience no more disease of their teeth and gums than patients on other practices in which I have worked where dry food was the norm. There is no dental benefit from dry food that even begins to offset the terrible harm done from feeding the wrong metabolic fuel to our cats."

Dr. Jean Hofve, Why Cats Need Canned Food

"Dry food is very dehydrating. Our feline friends descend from desert-dwelling wild cats who are well adapted to limited water resources. Their ultra-efficient kidneys are able to extract most of their moisture needs from their prey. However, the end result is that cats have a very low thirst drive, and will not drink water until they are 3-5% dehydrated (a level at which, clinically, a veterinarian would administer fluid therapy). Cats eating only dry food take in only half the moisture of a cat eating only canned food. This chronic dehydration may be a factor in kidney disease, and is known to be a major contributor to bladder disease (crystals, stones, FUS, FLUTD, cystitis)."

Anne Jablonski, Duke's Story: Inflammatory Bowel Disease

"Inflammatory bowel disease, with its attendant symptoms of diarrhea and vomiting, is the body's rebellion against trying to process foods it was never built to eat. A cat can never be a successful herbivore or omnivore and will never win any battle against digestive illness without consuming the enzyme-rich, meat-based food he or she was biologically engineered to ingest. Cats with IBD are desperate for biologically available nutrition while their increasingly exhausted bodies stay busy violently rejecting the inappropriate food that is moving through their compromised digestive tracts."

Dr. Michael Fox, Conflicts of Interest in the Veterinary Profession and the Origin of 'Man-Made' Dog and Cat Diseases

"Cats suffer more than dogs from poor nutrition because they are obligate carnivores requiring a meat-based diet. Too many veterinarians are profiting from selling dry cat foods high in cereals and soy; these only too often lead to obesity, diabetes mellitus, urinary tract and inflammatory bowel disease, and other chronic degenerative diseases. The veterinarians then profit from treating these diseases and from prescribing expensive special diets that would not be needed if the cats had been fed properly from the start."

CHAPTER THREE

Cats, Carbs & Calories

One of the most precious gifts many of us share is the affection of a cat (or two or three!). Unfortunately, feline life expectancy has been shrinking for over a decade. Obesity is now at epidemic levels for cats (and dogs), and many other preventable diseases are on the rise. The Banfield 2012 Pet Health Report five-year statistics show dramatic increases in several feline diseases, including a 15% climb in kidney disease, a 16% growth in diabetes mellitus, a significant 67% rise in arthritic cases, and an astonishing 90% leap in obesity. All of these diseases have links to diet and the first three are also linked to the fourth. It's no surprise, then, that feline obesity has become a huge concern to veterinarians and cat owners alike.

Why are so many cats getting fat?

There are several factors that impact a cat's body condition, including age, sexual status (intact or not), activity level, and metabolism, but the single most important – and overlooked – element in maintaining the domestic cat's weight is diet composition.

Although raw feeding is becoming increasingly more accepted, over 98% of today's housecats are still fed standard commercial diets, primarily kibble, and quite often on a free-feeding schedule. Kibble is a profoundly unhealthy diet for an obligate carnivore that evolved to have its water needs met through its food, but even more detrimental to feline health is the large carbohydrate content of many canned and the vast majority of kibble products (which require those ingredients to hold their form).

Like all obligate carnivores, cats have a digestive physiology that is uniquely and beautifully designed to harness the nutrients and calories from other animals to meet their nutritional and basic energy requirements. They have no dietary need for carbohydrates and, in fact, lack several of the metabolic pathways that would allow them to efficiently digest and utilize carbs. Furthermore, digested carbs are converted into glucose (or sugar) (Becker, Causes of Pet Diabetes) and – since cats are metabolically adapted for preferential use of animal protein and fat as energy sources (Zoran, Carnivore Connection) – typically stored as body fat. A high-carb diet provides a large number of calories that are destined to do no more than increase feline girth (and litter box usage!).

Conversely, cats readily and efficiently convert animal protein and fat into the energy they need to grow, maintain and repair every system in their bodies. Indeed, cats are so extraordinarily well-designed to process animal tissues that few of those calories are ever converted to body fat; you will rarely see an obese raw-fed cat.

In addition, animal protein – not food quantity – is the satiety trigger for cats. Until they ingest an adequate amount of recognizable animal protein, they will continue to feel hungry and, given the opportunity, will consume far more food than would otherwise be necessary.

Compounding this issue is the negative effect a high carb diet has upon protein absorption, requiring more food – and the concurrent ingestion of more carb calories – to satisfy the cats' hunger.

It's easy to see how today's predominately high carb, low protein cat foods almost invariably lead to feline obesity, and the pervasive practice of free-feeding just exacerbates the problem.

Why not just restrict caloric intake?

Restricting caloric intake without regard to diet composition is often effective in reducing weight in people, dogs and sometimes even cats, but it is ineffective as a long-term feline weight management solution for our domestic cats and can actually be detrimental to their health.

First, as already described, a calorie is not just a calorie to an obligate carnivore, and cats can consume more protein calories than carb calories without gaining weight (Winn study). In fact, if a cat is transitioned to a higher protein, lower carb diet, it will often begin losing weight even when the new diet contains a higher number of calories overall. Not only will the meat based calories provide the cat with necessary energy – while the calories from the carbs head primarily to fat storage – but cats on a high protein diet are more satisfied, energetic, and less anxious. Their higher levels of energy and wellbeing will also result in more play and a stronger overall physiology and immune system.

Of equal importance, cats have hepatic enzyme systems that are constantly active, requiring the catabolization of a fixed amount of dietary protein for energy no matter how much energy may also be available via carbs or fats. Let me emphasize this point – although cats can use some carbs for metabolic energy, their ability to swap protein utilization for carbs is so severely limited (Zoran, Carnivore Connection), they will cannibalize the protein in their own muscles to meet their basic daily needs if their diet does not contain enough, completely irrespective of how many carbs (or fat) they may also be eating. This is why my first dry food fed cat Lulu, who ate a main diet of kibble for 8+ years, never put on weight.

And this leads to the second reason: caloric restriction is ineffective and inappropriate for housecats. Most calorie-restrictive commercial products are high in fiber (a form of carbs) and do not contain enough protein to meet basic needs and preserve lean body mass. This decrease in muscle mass is an unhealthy weight loss state (especially worrying for senior cats) that will actually lower metabolism, make additional weight loss more difficult and increase the likelihood of a subsequent regain of body weight in fat.

In addition, fiber – not a naturally-occurring part of the cat's diet – blocks absorption of crucial nutrients into the small intestine, preventing the uptake of trace minerals, vitamins and antioxidants. Chronic nutrient deficiencies can lead to a host of diseases, not to mention a constantly hungry feline. These diets can lead to a cat that is concurrently overweight/underweight and nutritionally deficient. And not inclined to do much, beyond eat and sleep.

So what is the recommended solution?

Unfortunately, the pet food industry is not required to disclose the percentage of real meat in their products. Clearly, then, using recommended feeding allowances or calorie calculators to determine how much to feed a cat, especially one that needs to lose weight, is fairly futile.

The most optimal diet composition is roughly 52% protein, 46% fat and 2% carbs on a dry matter basis. Carb content is another bit of vital information most pet food products do not publish, but you can get a rough estimate of a product's carb content by adding the protein, fat, fiber, moisture and ash levels, subtracting that amount from 100, and dividing the result by the percentage of dry matter in the product.

For example, a product analysis that lists 50% protein, 22% fat, 2.80% fiber, 10% moisture, and .5% ash = 14.7 (100 – 85.3 (50 protein + 22 fat + 2.8 fiber + 10 moisture + .5 ash = 85.3) divided by .9 (100 – 10 moisture = 90% or .9) = 16.33% carbs. If this boggles you, you can use ChatGPT to calculate the carbs per DMB(Dry Matter Basis).

Your healthiest diet option, whether your kitty needs to lose weight or not, is a canned or raw diet that contains no or minimal amounts of fruits, grains or vegetables (less than 10% is good, less than 5% is better, none at all is best). Start by feeding about 4% of your cat's weight in ounces of canned food and 3% in raw per day, and then adjust the amount you feed based upon your cat's ongoing body condition.

Moving from free-feeding to offering three or four scheduled meals a day is also crucial to weight loss. Such a schedule more closely matches the cats' natural feeding pattern and has benefits that exceed weight management and include facilitating a digestive system that is healthy, strong, and working at peak efficiency.

Finally, increasing your cat's activity level will burn calories and increase lean muscle mass, effectively speeding up her metabolism. Daily interactive play sessions using wands, laser lights and other toys should be routine. Schedule these games for the same time every day and aim for dusk and dawn when the cats' natural hunting instincts are in high gear. Drag, dart, and hide the 'prey' to fully engage the cats' hunting behaviors and end each session by tossing the cat a healthy treat – such as freeze-dried meat – or a catnip toy to generate the satisfaction that accompanies a successful hunt.

In summary, routinely engaging your cat in play and offering her a fresh, raw diet that closely matches the nutrient composition she evolved to eat, on a schedule that more closely mimics her natural eating behavior, will almost certainly result in a healthier, more svelte and energetic version of her current self. Reducing or eliminating carbs is part of that equation, counting calories is not!

Can *You* afford to feed commercial raw?

In searching for the healthiest food to feed our cats, many people pass over the commercial raw option simply because they believe they can't afford it. And industry articles and blogs promote the notion that feeding commercially prepared raw food is the most expensive option. Finances are tight for many, and even those who adamantly desire the very best for their cats may be discouraged away from raw by these comments. My analysis completely debunks that myth. Raw is not, in fact, any more expensive to feed than other commercial options, and in many cases, it costs less!

For this analysis, I compared brands of kibble, canned foods, and commercial frozen raw foods.

Some of the results? If you're feeding a 4.5 Kg(10 Pound) cat the manufacturer recommended daily allowance (RDA), it's costing you approximately:

In kibble:

Whiskas/Meo Dry Food X 3 times a day: INR 60/day

Premium Grain Free Kibble: X 3 times a day : INR 150/day
In canned/wet food pouches:
Whiskas/Meo Wet Cat Food X 3 times a day: INR 273/day
Premium Wet cat Food(Royal Canin Instinctive Canned or similar): INR 1371/day
In raw:
I only found few sellers(see Sources & Resources at the end of the book) selling frozen raw cat and dog food in India. Based on the animal protein, their price for 1.5 kg of food ranges from Rs. 575.00(chicken) to Rs. 830/Kg(Beef and Turkey).

For brands that are not readily available in India, here's a price comparison:
The cheapest raw frozen food fed X 3 times daily costs at Rs. 250/day(Bravo Balance)
The most premium raw frozen food fed X 3 time daily costs Rs. 390/day(Vital Essentails frozen raw chicken)

<u>That's right; you can feed your cat a variety of frozen commercial raw food delivered to your door for less than it costs to feed Whiskas/Meo/Royal Canin wet food!</u>

According to Jane Brody, writing for The New York Times in 2010 (The Truth About Cat and Dog Food), "Recognizing the high value most owners place on their companion animals, and distressed by recent recalls of contaminated pet foods, two scientists decided to examine the pet food industry and the evidence for the value of its products and the claims made for them."

The results of the work of Marion Nestle, the Paulette Goddard Professor of nutrition, food studies and public health at New York University, and Malden C. Nesheim, Emeritus Professor of nutrition at Cornell University, were reviewed. The New York Times article reported that Dr. Nestle ("pronounced NES-sel") found "the so-called premium pet foods cost three to four times more than supermarket brands. Within the premium brands, there is also a wide price range yet when the ingredients lists are compared, they are strikingly similar. All pet foods are made from the byproducts of human food production. No matter what the package says, your dog/cat is not getting whole chicken breasts, but "what remains after the breasts have been removed for human food."

The NYT article lists the largest manufacturers in the pet food industry: Nestlé, Purina, Mars and Procter & Gamble. But Nestlé owns Purina (having purchased Ralston Purina in 2001), and Del Monte, which holds the #3 market share spot in the pet food industry, is not included in the list. Each of the pet food industry giants is first and foremost a giant in packaged human foods. The pet food industry giants are found in just about every isle of the supermarket – not just the pet supplies isle: pet food puts what would otherwise be profit-draining waste to profit-enhancing use.

Drs. Nestle and Nesheim examined premium versus non-premium brands and found that there often isn't much difference in quality. Given most pet foods are manufactured from the human food chain waste products, this shouldn't be overly surprising. They found that non-premium (generic or supermarket distribution) pet foods contain more grains and by-products, but that "all contained basically the same ingredients." Of course there are differences in protein sources, and marketing of "grain-free" foods has altered the pet food industry landscape forever. An apparent step in the right direction for a more species-appropriate diet, and certainly a life-saver for many pets that have developed allergies or other health problems related to consuming grains, sadly "grain-free" is not synonymous with low carbohydrates. It's no news to vets and animal nutritionists that cats, as carnivores, have essentially no nutritional requirement for carbohydrates. Yet those grains have been replaced with peas, potatoes, and other "non-grain" carbohydrates. Carrots, peas, and potatoes not fit for human consumption are still cheaper than human waste meat products.

The good news for people that want a convenient and affordable way to feed raw is that there is a sea of change occurring in the pet food industry, led by a transformation in our relationship with our pets and combined with growing consumer awareness. In 2006, Matthew Park, V.P. of Del Monte's Pet Products division said, "the humanization of pets is the single biggest trend driving our business." A report recently published by the Rockville, MD-based consumer research firm Packaged Facts, the U.S. Pet Market Outlook 2011-2012 indicates that currently over two-thirds (67%) of U.S. pet owners "strongly agree" that they consider their pets to be a part of the family. No wonder we do our best to buy the highest quality food we can afford!

Trade information indicates a growing number of pet owners are taking steps to provide better nutrition for their cats and dogs. According to the Packaged Facts' report, the "alternative" segment of pet food manufacturers is experiencing impressive growth despite the current economic environment. While the total U.S. pet food industry grew 0.5% in 2010, the fresh/frozen/refrigerated pet food category was one of the fastest growing segments. An established market, the fresh/frozen/refrigerated for dogs experienced 10% growth to $39.1 million; a relatively new commercial market, fresh/frozen/refrigerated for cats, grew a whopping 648.5% (off a nascent base) to approximately $1 million in sales.

The trend in raw feeding our pets is garnering a lot of attention in the pet food industry. PetfoodIndustry.com and other trade magazines and blogs have featured the growing demand for this healthier, species-appropriate food for our furry family members. Yet almost every article written about the subject implies the cost of feeding commercial raw food is essentially prohibitive. In an exchange with a vet writing for The Daily Vet blog, when the subject of feeding raw was raised in comments, his response was "I am a practitioner who participates in the real world where clients have economic realities that results in their feeding dry kibble so I offer advice to help them achieve goals with their choices without chastising them for their situation."

This piqued my curiosity. The cost of homemade raw is quite easy to calculate. Raw feeders use the guideline that cats require 2%-4% of their body weight in food daily; the only other required input – over which we have enormous control when making homemade food – is the amount we spend per pound of food purchased.

Assuming a 10 pound adult cat requires 2% of his body weight in food daily, the cost to feed one cat is:
At INR 84 per 1.5Kg of meat/bones/organs(chicken) the cost is INR 50 per day for 3 meals;
At INR 266 per 1.5 Kg of meat/bones/organs(antibiotic residue-free premium chicken) the cost is INR 100 per day for 3 meals;
At INR 251 per 1.5 Kg of meat/bones/organs(beef) the

cost is INR 150 per day for 3 meals;
At INR 333 per 1.5 Kg of meat/bones/organs(Quail)the cost is INR 200 per day for 3 meals;
At INR 417 per per 1.5 Kg of meat/bones/organs(Turkey)the cost is INR 250 per day for 3 meals
But how does this compare to commercial food options? The results were quite surprising.

The costs for daily feeding of premium/super-premium kibble ranges from INR 60 per day to INR 406 per day; for canned, from INR 243 to INR 1372 per day; for frozen raw (for instance, barfindia.com), from INR 160 to INR 976 per day. Yes, you read that right – it costs less to feed the most expensive commercial raw – shipped! – than the most expensive canned foods.

Because all kibble and canned foods can be purchased without shipping, those costs were not included. However, as most commercial raw foods if not available in local stores require shipping (and in some cases handling charges for the dry ice and special packaging), I compared commercial raw foods both with and without estimated shipping & handling charges. Comparisons were made assuming one 10 pound cat(4.5 Kg) and used recommended daily allowances(three meals).

To feed kibble, the approximate cost ranges from INR 40 per cat per day (Drools/Whiskas) to INR 258 for ND Grain-free and and INR 406 per day to feed ZiwiPeak's air-dried raw.

To feed canned, the cost ranges from INR 217 per cat per day (Whiskas Wet Adult Food) to INR 1374 (Royal Canin's Adult Instinctive Wet food).

To feed commercial raw excluding shipping, the cost ranges from INR 152 per cat per day (Nature's Menu frozen raw chicken) to INR 540 per day (Wild Kitty frozen raw chicken & clam).

To feed commercial raw including estimated shipping & handling charges(if you are in US), the cost ranges from INR 216 per cat per day (CountryPet Naturals frozen raw) to INR 600 (Wild Kitty).

It costs more than twice as much (239% as much!) to feed Royal Canin Adult Instinctive canned than it does the most expensive frozen raw food delivered to your door. And the cheapest commercial non-kibble option is a frozen raw food, not a canned food! As you can see, it is a complete myth that commercial raw costs more to feed your cat than canned food.

As this analysis illustrates so clearly, when evaluating the cost of FEEDING pet food, it is not sufficient to calculate the cost per pound. First, when feeding wet vs. dry, we pay for the moisture in canned food. It is almost by definition more expensive to feed than kibble because of this alone. Second, recommended feeding amounts vary quite widely due to the differing nutritional content of the foods. Thus the recommended quantity of food to be fed daily is an essential factor in calculating daily feeding cost.

For kibble, recommended daily amounts (RDA) for one 10 pound cat(4.5 Kg) range from 1.6 ounces daily (Hill's Science Diet Ideal Balance Adult Feline) to approximately 4.2 ounces daily (California Natural Chicken Grain-Free). Because of the moisture content in canned food, the RDA of wet food ranges from 4.1 ounces (PRO PAC Superpremium Adult Cat Food) to 13.8 ounces (9 Lives Daily Essentials).

The most expensive food per pound, *Rad Cat* frozen raw food, per pound (including estimated shipping and handling) actually costs LESS to feed than PurinaOne SmartBlend canned or Royal Canin Adult Instinctive, at INR 497 and INR 733 per pound, respectively. And if your local retailer carries or can order Nature's Menu frozen raw, Aunt Jeni's frozen raw, Bravo Balance frozen raw, or Darwin's Pet Naturals frozen raw (each reflects chicken variety), ALL of these cost less to feed your cat daily than the cheapest canned food option (PRO PAC).

I feel it is also important to note that there are commercial raw options cost less than feeding kibble! There are 3 commercial raw foods (excluding shipping) that cost less to feed (Nature's Menu Chicken, $0.61 per day; Aunt Jeni's chicken, $0.67 per day; Bravo Balance chicken, $0.68 per day) than 2 of the most expensive kibbles (California Natural Grain-Free Dry, $0.75 per day; and Newman's Own Organics Adult Dry, $0.75 per day).

As to the grain-free options? Grain-free does not always mean low carbohydrates and more meat and protein. This is not news. Cats are carnivores and have no dietary requirement for carbohydrates. A recent study, "Estimation of the dietary nutrient profile of free-roaming feral cats: possible implications for nutrition of domestic cats," (Plantinga et al. 2011) published last October, is an analysis of the nutritional content of feral cat diets – 27 studies, 6,666 data points.

The study confirms what we already know: cats eat raw meat. The study found that the hunting feral cats consumed approximately 2% carbs (N-free extract, "NFE"), and all NFE consumption was incidental ingestion, meaning the stomach contents of consumed prey animals. So how do our commercial foods fare in providing species-appropriate nutrition? All carbohydrate content presented on a dry-

matter basis:
The 48 kibble products analyzed ranged from 7% carbohydrates to 43% carbs. Of the 19 grain-free kibble foods compared in the analysis, just 4 have less than 10% carbohydrates, and one of those is an all meat air-dried raw. The lowest carb content of a grain-free kibble is 7%; the highest carb content of a grain-free kibble is a shocking 41%.

Wet foods fared better. The 40 wet foods analyzed ranged from 1.8% carbohydrates to 29.9% carbs. Of 17 grain-free brands of wet food analyzed, 6 have less than 10% carbs. Interestingly, 6 supermarket/pet store/ specialty distribution brands that are not grain-free (or not marketed as grain-free) also have less than 10% carbs.

The commercial raw products aren't marketed as grain-free foods. But not surprisingly, none had in excess of 10% carbohydrates: most have just 0.5% carbohydrates.

The bottom line? There are raw feeding options (both commercial and homemade) that are cost competitive to feeding kibble and canned. If you live in the U.S. and can afford to feed an inexpensive canned food or an expensive kibble, you have a couple of commercial raw feeding options. If you live in India, the resources section has a few sources or you can learn how to make your cat's food from scratch, like I do.

CHAPTER FOUR

The Grocery Store Dilemma

Standing in line at the grocery store watching customers purchase a bag of dry, bargain brand cat or dog food is very hard for me. All I want to do is grab the bag and start explaining the health risks they are taking home to their companion.

I've stopped myself from handing over a business card on a number of occasions, recognizing I doubt the store would appreciate me soliciting their customers. But am I abandoning a good opportunity? Do good intentions grant a waiver of poor business manners?

Me: "Pardon me, are you aware the dry food you are purchasing may be causing or can cause your cat health issues, especially urinary problems?

Customer: "But he loves this stuff! And my vet says to feed him what he'll eat."

Me: "You do realize it's flavored to addict him? Manufacturers have to because the ingredients are the opposite of what a cat's natural diet would be. You know, such as mice and birds, high in moisture and meat protein?"

Customer: "I won't let my cat outside, that's why I give him this indoor food."

Store Cashier: "Ladies, you are holding up the line."

Me: "Your cat is a carnivore, an animal who requires high meat protein and the food you are holding probably only contains 20% meat tops."

Customer: "See, it says, 'Made with real chicken meat'."

Me: "Misleading. Read the ingredient panel on the back."

Store Cashier: "Please, you two need to move on. (To me) Ma'am, this customer is trying to leave. Do I need to call a store manager?"

Me: "No. It's just difficult when I know so many pets can become ill because of species inappropriate diets."

Store Cashier: (To customer) "Don't forget your litter."

Me: (Gasp to myself . . . it's scented litter. No, no, no, no, no!). (See this Dr Karen Becker's video on cat litter to learn what's the best litter to buy)

This encounter made me wonder:

- Is it budget concerns that make pet parents reach for an economy store brand or is it lack of knowledge?
- Are they aware of the potential costs to their animal's health with inappropriate foods?
- Do owners understand there is a difference in ingredient

quality and manufacturing practices?

- All pet foods are not the same and good pet food does not have to be expensive.

There are *okay* foods in the grocery aisle and many you can order online right from home, you just need to know your pet's dietary requirements and how to read a label to help your companion on its way to better health and nutrition. There are a lot of myths about cat food and how to feed cats. You will hear some of these in real life, probably from your own vet or animal rescuer.

10 Cat Food Myths

Myth #1: Dry food is the best food for cats.

Once considered the end-all and be-all for feline nutrition, evidence now shows dry foods may be a source of chronic health issues. Urinary, arthritis, kidney, diabetes, and dental problems are just a few of the diseases now associated with dry food diets, including those that are grain free. Water matters and is most absorbable and beneficial in food. Moisture rich foods offer critical support to electrolyte and micronutrient balance, helping maintain cellular membranes throughout the body. Quality canned, raw, and well-balanced home-made foods offer higher meat proteins, fewer carbohydrates, proper moisture levels, and fewer highly processed ingredients, mimicking a more natural diet.

Myth #2: Dry food is important for cleaning teeth.

Your cat is an obligate carnivore with teeth designed for tearing and shredding, not grinding. Because of the size and texture, most dry foods are swallowed whole with minimal chewing. What little of these carbohydrate rich foods is chewed, produces a starchy film that adheres to teeth creating a rich environment for dental-damaging bacteria.

Myth #3: Premium Wet foods are just higher priced foods.

The adage – you get what you pay for – is just as true with pet foods. Nutrition is not only about whether your cat likes and eats the food, but how digestible the food is, what your cat can absorb, and how your cat metabolizes it. Some premium food manufacturers(such as some Raw Frozen Food suppliers) go to great lengths to source quality ingredients, cook at low temperatures to preserve valuable nutrients, and use special packaging to preserve freshness. Inexpensive foods should raise alarms; corners were cut either in the ingredients, manufacturing, storage or labor.

Myth #4: Do not mix or change cat foods.

In the wild, your feline predator will hunt for a range of entrees from mice to bugs. A well-planned variety of foods may prevent over-supplementation, nutritional imbalances, and the development of food sensitivities. Slow introductions of a selection of foods with a variety of proteins, textures and styles, will encourage better digestion, a healthier immune system, and help reduce fixation on select foods.

Myth #5: Organic cat foods are superior.

While organic and free-range meats make superior protein sources, they are often not the primary ingredients in commercial organic pet foods. Because of costs, many dry and some canned foods use higher levels of plant proteins to meet nutritional requirements, increasing the carbohydrate load in your cat's diet. Cats cannot properly metabolize high volumes of carbohydrates and in turn store them as fat. Understanding your cat's nutritional needs

AND how to read labels will help you select the best foods for your obligate carnivore.

Myth #6: Diet foods offer better weight management. Increased fiber and empty calorie ingredients are used in lite, indoor and weight management diets. These ingredients add to the load of carbohydrates and can actually contribute to weight gain, trigger skin and coat disorders, and create food intolerances. Be aware, grain-free does not equate to carb free. A water-rich, meat-based, low-carbohydrate diet – canned, raw, or home-cooked – that is balanced for your cat's caloric needs, is the key to a sleek and agile cat.

Myth #7: People food and homemade foods are harmful to cats.
If you have a feline audience when preparing your meals, know that you and your cat can eat a number of the same things you eat: meat, fish, eggs, and a small amount of veggies/fruit/psylium. Break the dependence on commercial foods and discover the health benefits of fresh, homemade cat food your cat will pounce on. A well-balanced, home-prepared diet using free range meats and fresh organic ingredients you source are the best foods for you and your cat because it gives you control over recipes, supplements, and processing. Adding even a little fresh food can go a long way to boosting the nutritional value of your cat's diet.

Myth #8: Raw foods have the highest risk of bacterial contamination.
As a predator, your cat evolved with a digestive tract designed to process and eliminate food quickly—short, acidic, and hostile to bacteria. While caution should be taken with cats with weakened immune systems or in homes with humans with health challenges, proactive

procedures of leading manufacturers of raw diet pet foods offer safety and peace of mind.

Myth #9: Food must be left out, so your cat won't go hungry.

Leaving dry food out is for our convenience, not the health of your cat. Dry foods are sprayed with flavorings to addict your cat. The more your cat eats, the more it wants, discouraging your cat from other foods. Unless there is a specific health issue, cats benefit from a schedule of 3-4 small meals a day for more complete and proper digestion. A couple of snacks are fine but remember that's a few pieces . . . not a bowlful.

Myth #10: Diet does not affect stress, aggression, or hyperactivity.

Behavior issues can be affected by a range of ingredients in the diet, from the type of protein—meat vs. plant—to carbohydrates, in addition to the level of processing. Cats are especially susceptible to the balance of amino acids and micronutrients. Food sensitivities can also be at the root of behavior issues. When working with any behavior issue, it's imperative the diet is evaluated. Foods aren't only about calories and energy; a species appropriate cat diet nourishes their body, brain, and every other organ system.

Do Lions & Tigers Get Hairballs?

What are hairballs? How do they develop? Are they just innocuous or can they be life threatening? How often is normal for a cat to bring up a hairball? And what can we do to prevent our cats from developing them? For those of you who've had the experience of stepping on that slimy, cigar-shaped deposit and frustrated by on-going issues, maybe my pursuit of questions will offer some relief for you and your cat.
When cats groom themselves or other cats, they ingest the fur due to the backward-slanted projections (papillae) on their tongue that pulls in loosened hair and directs it down the throat to be swallowed. Since hair is indigestible, it should then pass through the digestive tract and get eliminated through feces. If hair remains and is not emptied from the stomach, then it begins to mix with gastric secretions and food, accumulating into a sponge like texture. The unique cigar like shape only develops from being expelled through the esophagus and they can be an inch to 5 inches in length. If the hairball becomes too large to vomit up or pass, or gets lodged in the GI tract, then surgery is required. So yes, hairballs can become life-threatening.

When should you become alarmed? Through all my research, I was overwhelmed with the volumes on hairball elimination recommendations but found extraordinarily little on causes and prevention. Articles offered quotes that ranged from "It's not uncommon to regurgitate a hairball once or twice a week," to "once or twice a year isn't normal." There are scads of remedies, foods, and treats to help your cat eliminate. But to get to the root of hairballs and prevention, I started by asking if their big cat cousins got hairballs.

> "*"Even though cats of all sizes groom themselves the same way, hairballs are 'not a normal thing in big cats,' captive or not," Matthew Johnson, an associate professor at Colorado State University's Veterinary Teaching Hospital commented in the National Geographic story Do Big Cats Get Hairballs? Hairballs may be attributed to an underlying gastrointestinal problem, like inflammatory bowel disease. However, a controversial topic is whether commercial foods can trigger digestive issues, says Johnson. He goes on to explain big cats in zoos and reserves such as jaguars and leopards get meat and animal carcasses—a species appropriate diet while smaller wildcats, such as servals or ocelots living in captivity, are often fed a domestic cat-type of diet. "This may explain why the smaller wild cats occasionally vomit up hairballs," Johnston offers.*"

If hairballs aren't normal. It makes you think what other cat issues we've dusted off as a species' issue is actually a diet/overvaccination issue. Many cat health issues which we think is 'normal' species' behaviour are in fact not. Even zoomies may not be natural and cats may use them to work off the excess carbs they consumed from kibble. Nature designed cats perfectly, it's us who have lost our ways of tending to their needs correctly.

Internally, your cat is not different from its wild cousins.

CHAPTER FIVE

Why Cats are the way they are

Because cats are so often portrayed by the pet industry as prima donnas, cuddly couch potatoes, or aloof manipulators, cat owners have a poor understanding of the animal living with them. The best way to describe them: Cats are ultimate survivalists and that's what makes them so remarkable.

Felis Silvestris Catus has changed little from its ancestors: anatomically, behaviorally, and metabolically. Their stealth and highly efficient predator physiology, while helping protect them from danger and starvation in the wild, can also set them up for stress and anxiety, even fear in a household setting. Their hearing, which allows them to listen in and track ultrasonic sounds of rodents and small prey, goes on overload or perceives a range of sounds found in the home environment as potential threats: electronics, electromagnetic frequencies, loud noises, unusual sounds, or neighboring animals. Paw pads, attuned to picking up vibrations when honing in on prey, also absorb unknown environmental vibrations, placing the animal on alert for a potential encounter. Isolated, the cat may startle with these events, recovering easily. If the environmental events are ongoing then the cat is at risk of health and/or behavior issues. In fact, there is growing evidence many chronic health problems of domestic cats are directly or indirectly the result of stressors or unusual environmental events.

African wild cat(Felis Silvestris Catus)

European Wildcat(*Felis Silvestris Catus*)

The domestic Cat(*Felis catus*)

Only recently, due to these increased health and behavioral issues, science has started looking at how cats relate to their surroundings: the home environment, their humans and, other animals. So, in addition to its distinctive physiology, we need to consider the cat's environment and its perceived lack of control. Unusual or threatening scents, unfamiliarity of a caregiver or new surroundings, change in routines, hierarchies with other animals, even the rearrangement of furnishings can place a cat on the edge. Territory security is critical for cats, some say more so than their attachment to humans.

However, a cat's perception of safety is filtered by certain factors:

1. Was the cat introduced to humans during that fragile socialization window as a kitten? Or is the cat guarded from humans and grew up feral?
2. Is the cat encouraged to explore (with supervision) to help build confidence? Or is the cat more locked away and isolated? A less confident cat can find itself at the mercy of a stressful lifestyle.
3. And what about the human-feline relationship? A recent study supports what cat owners have known– cats do develop deep attachments, create a language just for their humans, respond to our emotions, and can even recognize facial expressions. Our human-animal relationship and how we assemble as part of their territory is just as critical.

Unless we are feeding a species-appropriate diet to these obligate carnivores, it's akin to us using cheap fuel in our vehicles. It will run, but how well? Good nutrition is the most important factor in health and longevity. But what's not often discussed is how poor nutrition influences behavior. Many commercial cat foods are increasingly using plant proteins to meet the higher protein needs of cats. Unfortunately, plant proteins do not offer the complete amino acid profile required by this carnivore and must be balanced accordingly. While supplementation may look good on the label, our cats are the test subjects for long-term nutritional balancing. In my experience, foods can be deficient in or have less bioavailable stress-fighting nutrients found naturally in the cat's carnivore diet. These can include, taurine and arginine, Vitamin Bs, Vitamin C, Magnesium, Zinc, and phytonutrients, which help reduce anxiety and normalize stress responses. Rotation of diet and type of meats should also be at the forefront. Variety protects against boredom, fixation, and nutrient imbalances.

More recently, I have been looking at the gut-brain axis, the feline microbiome, as well as the support of medicinal mushrooms and energy medicine modalities such as homeopathy. How can we incorporate the synergy of these therapies to treat the whole cat? For instance, stress and anxiety are known triggers for house soiling, yet, rarely looked at as a contributing factor to gastrointestinal issues and other sickness behaviors, which can include decreased food and water intake, anorexia, vomiting, diarrhea, respiratory infections, decreased activity, and social interactions, and reduced body care (grooming). We understand from human research that the brain can affect the GI microbiome neurologically and hormonally by changing intestinal motility, permeability, pH, and mucus secretion throughout the length of the intestine or regionally. Reciprocally, healthy GI development is essential to the development of the central nervous system. Herbal therapies offer healing support through medicinal properties from nose to tail and all organ systems, and on a supportive role nutritional benefits add yet another healing dimension. Mushroom blends add the nutritional values of added vitamins, minerals, and antioxidants. And in theory, we tapped into the cellular to cellular connections of the Common Mycorrhizal Network to help the cat feel more grounded in an indoor-only environment(see the work of mycologist Paul Stamets).

Feline well-being requires us to acknowledge the cat's innate nature and physiology. We must respect their need for security and safety in their territories and enrich their environments. We need to encourage social contact and supervised explorations, but with an understanding of their innate requirements and at times on their terms. We should offer hunting and predatory enactments for mental and physical activity, and last but not least, offer a species-appropriate diet. All these criteria are just as important as loving and petting.

We are modern zookeepers.

> "*The cat, it is well to remember, remains the friend of man because it pleases him to do so and not because he must.*
> *-CARL VAN VECHTEN (1880–1964) AMERICAN WRITER AND PHOTOGRAPHER*"

Today's domestic cats are probably all descended from the wildcat Felis silvestris lybica, a species native to the Middle East. It's estimated that there may now be half a billion domestic cats around the world, at a time when the existence of the other 36 or so species of wildcat is threatened or endangered. Pet cats are amazingly adept at occupying two seemingly parallel universes. Within one neat furry package there coexists a well-armed, ruthless nocturnal hunter and a beguiling, manipulative, purring cat. One can terrorize the local rodent and bird populations; the other can wrap you around its long tail and knows all the right buttons to push and heartstrings to tug to live a life of cosseted luxury. Being able to read your cat's body language and interpret its meowing simply means you can anticipate its mood and desires more swiftly and accurately.

The cat has followed humans for about 10,000 years, tagging along from primitive farming communities to the urban jungle. The earliest example of a domestic cat was found in a Neolithic grave on Cyprus, among the dead of people who probably brought the animal from Turkey. It has been dated to about 7500 B.C., which links to the origins of agriculture. By about 2000 B.C., when the Egyptians realized how useful the cat was in protecting their grain (see page 64), they had invited the cat into their homes—or, more likely, the cat adopting the humans instead of the humans adopting the cat.

Two ratters given to a Huron Indian chief might have been the first cats in North America. Sadly, they died without producing kittens. Some think the domestic cat arrived on the Mayflower. In 1749, cats were imported from England to control the rats.

10 Countries With The Most Pet Cats

One unofficial estimate puts the total cat population in the United States at around 93 million, based on 63 million pet cats and about 30 million feral cats—ferals are the wild offspring of domestic cats, which by definition are hard to count. Some people feel that this is a gross underestimation and would guestimate that there could be one feral for every pet cat in the country. Cats have overtaken dogs as the most popular pet in the United States.

COUNTRY	NUMBER OF CATS
United States	76,430,000
China	53,100,000
Russia	12,700,000
Brazil	12,466,000
France	9,600,000
Italy	9,400,000
Great Britain	7,700,000
Ukraine	7,350,000
Japan	7,300,000
Germany	7,200,000

TOP TEN COUNTRIES WITH THE MOST PET CATS

Population Explosion

If left to her own devices, a female cat can have three to seven kittens every four months. Theoretically, in five years, one un-neutered female cat can have over 20,000 descendants. One pair of breeding cats and their offspring can produce over 400,000 new cats in seven years. Unlike humans, female cats do not have a menopause and remain fertile throughout their lives, unless neutered.

A cat called Dusty, living in Bonham, Texas, was 17 years old when she gave birth to her 420th kitten on June 23, 1952.

In 1987, a cat called Kitty, owned by George Johnstone of Croxton, Staffordshire, England, produced a litter of two kittens—at the magnificent age of 30! Kitty died 2 years later, at the age of 32.

One in four pregnant cats carries kittens fathered by more than one mate. A fertile female may mate with several tomcats, which fertilize different eggs each time, which is why kittens in the same litter can have different colors and coats.

> "*No matter how much cats fight, there always seems to be plenty of kittens?*
> *- ABRAHAM LINCOLN (1809–65), 16TH PRESIDENT OF THE UNITED STATES*"

A sexually active feral tomcat lays claim to an area of about 3 square miles (8 sq km) and sprays strategic points with strong smelling urine to mark his territory. Most cats killed on the road are un-neutered toms, because they are more likely to roam farther afield and cross busy roads.

Warm temperatures are responsible for a feline population explosion. As the winters become shorter and milder, cats start breeding earlier and there is less of a lull in kitten production.

The Aging Cat

Cats, like people, are living longer than ever. Here's a comparison of how a cat ages in comparison to a human. Of course, also like people, cats age at different rates, depending on their genes, epigenetics and environmental factors.

CAT'S AGE	EQUIVALENT HUMAN AGE	COMPARISONS
2–3 months	9–12 months	Weaned and becoming more independent.
4 months	2–3 years	Children mobile and talking; kittens completely independent of mother.
6–12 months	12–15 years	Kitten and adolescent are both sexually mature but may still be growing.
2 years	24 years	Completely independent—if your lucky.
3–6 years	28–40 years	Human career and family building.
6–9 years	40–52 years	Creeping middle-age spread; some women have already entered menopause.
9–13 years	52–65 years	Retirement looms; cats begin to slow down, too.
13–17 years	65–85 years	Still active but getting older: less agile mentally and physically; injuries heal more slowly; internal organs less efficient.
17–19 years	83–92 years	Increasingly frail: hearing, sight, and mobility deteriorating; bones thinning; less fat; delicate skin; less supple; weaker muscle tone.
19–22 years	92–100 years	Declining years.
22+ years	100+ years	More and more cats and humans are reaching this venerable age.
30 years	136 years	Now cats outstrip humans; several have reached this age.
34–36 years	152–160 years	Officially oldest cat. According to Guinness World Records, the oldest cat was Creme Puff, who lived to 37; he belonged to Jake Perry of Austin, Texas.
43 years	188 years	Unverified cat claim.

Cats and their equivalent Human Age

ANATOMICAL FACTS

The cat has a reflective tissue at the back of its eyes to increase the light reaching the retina—this is also what makes a cat's eyes glow in the dark. Contrary to popular belief, cats cannot see in total darkness.

A cat's hearing ability is five times that of a human. A dog has a greater range of pitch, but a cat's hearing exceeds a dog's for high-pitched sounds, such as the squeak of a mouse. Cats can and do hear ultrasonic sounds that precede a noisy event, such as an earthquake or storm.

Although a cat's sense of smell is much better than a human's, it's not as developed as a dog's. However, it is fully developed at birth, and a kitten can tell the difference between its mother's nipples and those of another cat by their smell.

All of an adult cat's 30 teeth are designed to shred meat—instead of chewing food, they chop it. The large canines, or fangs, are used to break the necks of their prey. It's reckoned that cats are responsible for killing 566 million birds each year.

A cat's whiskers are basically thick hairs with well-developed sensory organs. Each side of the cat's nose has a set of 12 whiskers, which are normally as long as the widest part of the cat's body—unless it is obese or pregnant. The whiskers can detect nearby movement, which is handy when hunting in the dark.

Just like humans are often left-handed or right-handed, cats have a preferred front paw. Only 20 percent are right-pawed, while 40 percent are left-pawed and the remaining 40 percent are ambidextrous.

There is no firm consensus on the mechanism of the purr. Some say it originates in the larynx (voice box) when a second pair of vocal chords start vibrating; others believe it is generated by blood flow resonating in the wind pipe and nasal cavities.

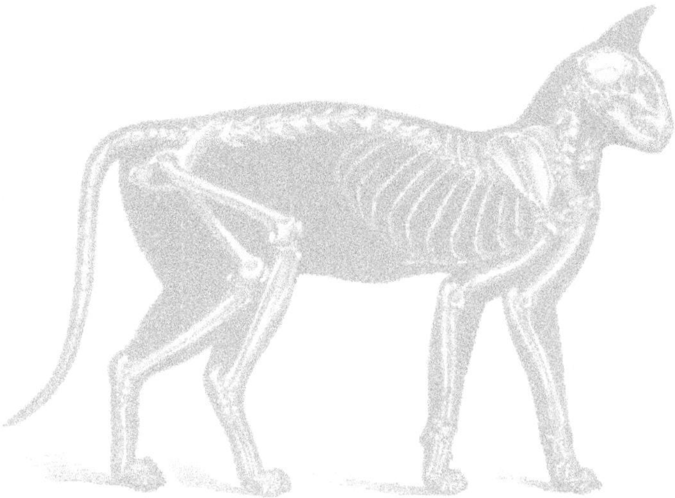

Physical Anatomy of a Cat

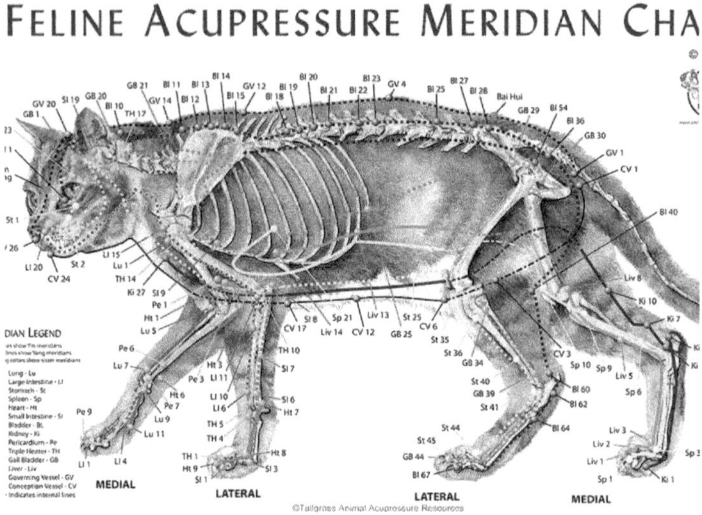

Energetic Anatomy of a Cat

FURRY FRIENDS

Most cats have true fur, which means they have both a soft, fine undercoat and a long, coarser outer coat. A cat sheds its fur when it spends more time in light—which is why an outdoors cat sheds its coat in spring, when there is more daylight, until fall, when daylight is shorter. House cats also shed because of exposure to light from lightbulbs and even appliances, such as the television.

A nerve is connected to each hair in a cat's coat. When stroked, there is a decrease in the cat's muscle tension and heart rate—which is, funnily enough, what also happens to the person stroking the cat.

If you sneeze whenever you're around cats, it's probably not the cat hair that irritates your nose, but the saliva that remains on their fur. Cat saliva contains a detergent that keeps their fur clean. While this is great for the cat, it isn't for people who are allergic to cats. If the resident cat is bathed and groomed regularly, allergic people can sometimes tolerate it better.

Studies now show that the allergen in cats is also related to their scent glands. Cats have scent glands on their faces and at the bottom of their tails. Un-neutered male cats generate the most scent. If this secretion from the scent glands is the allergen, allergic people should tolerate spayed female cats the best.

THE TABBY

The tabby is not a distinct breed of cat but a coat pattern that can appear in all breeds. It most closely resembles the pattern on the cat's wild ancestor. The word "tabby" stems from attabi, which describes the swirling markings on silk fabrics woven in the Attabiya district of Baghdad in Iraq.

Classic or blotched tabby has bold, swirling patterns of dark and lighter circular smudges arranged like a bull's-eye on its sides.

Ticked tabby, sometimes called an Abyssinian or agouti tabby, doesn't have any traditional stripes or spots on its body, so it doesn't look much like a tabby. However, its coat has tabby markings on the face and agouti hairs on the body. Agouti hairs are best seen in the lighter parts of a tabby's coat, where you'll see that the individual hairs are striped with alternating light and dark bands.

Mackerel tabby, sometimes known as a tiger cat, has narrow parallel stripes down the sides of its body. The best stripes are evenly spaced, unbroken lines that branch from one stripe running along the spine like a fish skeleton, which is why the pattern is described as mackerel.

Spotted tabby has spots all over its sides. They may be large or small, round, oval, or rosette, and they sometimes appear to be broken mackerel stripes. A mackerel tabby with a broken stripe pattern can look a lot like a spotted tabby.

Patched tabby is used to describe a tortoiseshell tabby. Typically, the cat's coat has separate patches of brown tabby and red tabby. A tortoiseshell carrying the tabby gene is often called a tortie. Patched tabbies can show any of the four distinct tabby patterns. The markings are usually more apparent on the legs and head.

A Coat Of Many Colors

An orange cat may be just an orange cat to most people, but to cat breeders its coat is red, to children's story writers, it's marmalade, to British people it's ginger, and, in the old days, it would have been called yellow.

The gene in cats that causes the orange coat color is sex linked, and carried on the X sex chromosome. This gene may show itself as orange or black. A male cat, with only one X chromosome, can be only orange or black, but not both. A female cat with two X chromosomes may have both orange and black colors in its coat, which is why almost all tortoiseshell cats are female.

It is extremely rare to come across a male cat with both orange and black in his coat. To have both the orange and the black coat colors, the male cat must have all or part of both female X chromosomes. This unusual sex chromosome combination would make him sterile.

When a six-month-old tortoiseshell stray was brought into the Escondido Humane Society in San Diego, California, to be spayed, the veterinarian was shocked. Phinny—short for Phenomenon, as the cat became known—turned out to need neutering because "she" was a "he." Male torties are rarely seen and Phinny was a genuine genetic anomaly.

Common names for cats with White Markings

A cat that has ...	is said to be ...
white paws	mitted(called Mittens')
a white patch on its chest	a locket cat
small white patches on its belly	buttons
a roughly half-white coat	bicolor
a mostly white coat with a few color patches	harlequin
a black coat with white legs, underside, and chest	a tuxedo cat
a black-and-white coat	a jellicle cat

Taxonomy of Cats

CHAPTER SIX

Salmonella, E. Coli & Listeria, Oh My!

The two most common fears that raw feeding neophytes have involve bones and bacteria. Today, we're going to focus on the big bad spectre - bacteria and other pathogens.

Bacteria are everywhere. They are a natural part of our ecosystems and can be found from the depths of the oceans to the heights of the mountains. They are in the soil, in the air, and in the bodies of all animals – including ours. Bacteria are an integral part of the health of this planet and as such, are inescapable.

Potentially dangerous bacteria are in our food chain; as evidenced by several recent recalls, in both veggies and meat supplies. Every food we offer our cats has some level of health risk. The question lies not in whether such risks exist, but in the quantification of those risks. Raw meat can be contaminated with bacteria, but kibble can be contaminated with the same pathogens(albeit in a more drug and heat resistant form) and contains the added dangers of fungus and mold toxins, which have killed and sickened many pets. The Center for Disease Control recommends that pet owners not feed pets in the kitchen or wash pets‘ food and water dishes in the kitchen sink or the bathtub, though no such warning has been issued for the daily preparation of the family's home-cooked chicken or steak dinner.

Commercially-produced cat foods also contain the risks of inadvertent vitamin deficiency or toxicity (or both!), not to mention the quality control issues inherent in the pet food industry's processing practices. The 2007 pet food poisoning horror is a prime example of such potential contamination.

So what's a cat owner to do?

Why, we provide our cat the fuel her high-performance gastrointestinal system is designed to run on. As an obligate carnivore, she is uniquely, specifically and extraordinarily well designed to thrive on the tissues and bones and organs of prey animals, and that is exactly what we should be feeding her. It is the diet that contains the consistently highest-quality nutritional profile and the lowest risk of contaminants.

Ah, but what about those pesky, potentially harmful pathogens?

As difficult as it may be to believe, it is a basic premise of natural science that cats, like all animals, are born with the tools and conditions necessary to maintain their health. In this case, cats have evolved a natural and effective defense against the bacteria found in their foods and environment. It starts right in their mouths, with a salivary enzyme called lysozyme. This enzyme attacks bacteria and other pathogens, and can even neutralize bacteria on their fur during grooming. In India there is a 'myth‘ that if a cat scratches you you need to let them lick the spot you got the scratch on! It sounds ridiculous, but maybe some of our ancestors knew about this anti-bacterial enzyme in cat's saliva. I'm not recommending you try this, but it's an interesting anecdote. For a cat scratch or bite, just wash and clean the area with the scratch and dab with a few drops of antiseptic tincture such as *Calendula*. You don't need to take a rabies shot and compromise yours or your pet's immune system. Kittens don't usually bite unless they are teethings or stressed/around unfamiliar cats; the biting is a survival response that's built in as a self-defense mechanism in such situations.

Bacteria that make it past the mouth hit an extremely acidic stomach that contains hydrochloric acid and several digestive enzymes; an environment deadly to these pathogens. Once past the stomach and into the small intestine, bacteria encounter additional obstacles, including strong antimicrobial agents in the form of bile salts from the liver. The pancreas secretes more enzymes as well as bicarbonate, which breaks down the cell walls of invading bacteria. After the small intestine, digestive matter passes through the large intestine, where high levels of beneficial bacteria flourish. This natural intestinal flora competes with any surviving pathogens for resources, preventing them from taking hold and forcing them out of the body. Lysozyme, the initial gate-keeper, is also present throughout the digestive tract and is expelled right along with the cat's waste. All of this happens very quickly, disallowing pathogens time to multiply.

Comparatively-speaking, cats have one of the shortest digestive tracts in the animal kingdom. Their body length-to-digestive tract ratio is only 1:4, compared to 1:6 for the dog (and us!), and 1:20 for the cow. Animal-based meals take on average only 12 hours to pass completely through.

Several studies have shown an intimate relationship between the cat's natural diet and the animal's intestinal characteristics; what a cat eats affects how that food is digested.

The latest edition of The Nutrient requirements of dogs and cats by the National Research Council Ad Hoc Committee on Dog and Cat Nutrition goes into great depth examining the complexities of this relationship. From the amount and composition of saliva secreted during the meal to the activity of stomach and intestinal enzymes and other digestive secretions to the speed at which food is moved through the digestive tract, high protein / high moisture diets have a beneficial to the health of body and mind. Eating a raw diet is not only good for the cat from a nutritional perspective – it causes a chain reaction of chemical events that actively increases the cat's natural defenses against pathogens.

Fleas? Pfft.

According to Dr. Celeste Yarnall, the cat's body is so efficient at managing bacteria that it destroys approximately 98% of the pathogens it ingests. 98%! That's as effective as America's most popular cleaning solutions!

From the enzymes in their saliva to their internal chemical reactions to the short transit time, healthy cats truly are well equipped for eating the raw animal diets upon which they are so beautifully designed to thrive.

Tests show that human stomach acid pH ranges from 1.5 - 3.5 post prandial(after a meal). Dogs' stomach pH ranged from 1.05 - 2.2. For cats it's 2-2.5. It is possible that humans who eat a meat based diet have stronger stomach acid than some kibble-fed dogs. But on an average, pH in dogs and cats stomachs is slightly stronger than human stomach acid.

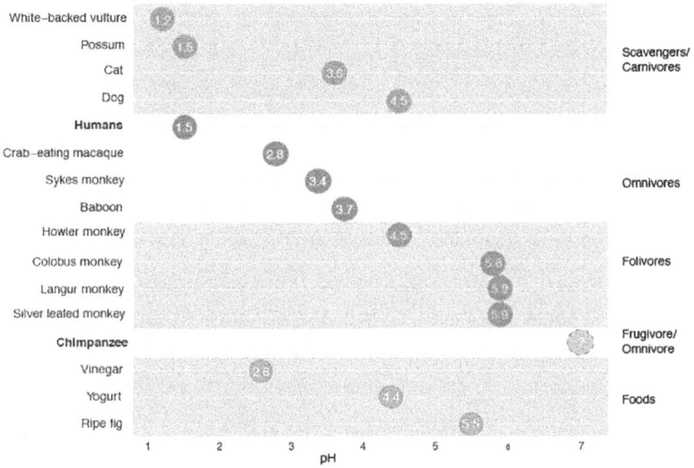

This table above shows the average pH across species.

Raw Feeding Health-compromised cats (IBD, FIV+, etc.)

One of the two most common concerns of cat owners contemplating the switch to a fresh diet is the specter of potentially lethal bacteria; the other is the fear of bones. We discussed how easily and thoroughly healthy cats manage the bacteria in their environment, including in their foods. But what about feeding a diet with potentially harmful bacteria to a cat that **isn't** healthy, or one with a compromised immune system, such as an FIV+?

My answer to the query, “Can you feed raw foods to a cat whose health is compromised in some manner?” is “Yes!” Cats are so finely-tuned for a diet of prey animals that it’s not only safe to put FIV+ cats on a raw diet, it’s vitally important to support their immune systems by feeding them the foods that are going to nourish their physiology at the highest and most efficient levels.

The latest edition of The Nutrient requirements of dogs and cats by the National Research Council (U.S.) Ad Hoc Committee on Dog and Cat Nutrition goes into great depth examining the complexities of the relationships between the cat's digestive physiology and chemical workings and the foods it eats. It cites studies proving the cat's entire digestive system functions at a higher level of efficiency when fed a raw diet; beginning right at the mouth – more saliva, with a more efficient composition of enzymes, is produced during a meal of raw, animal-based foods. The stomach acids are different, the pacing through the system is different, the enzymes released from the various organs (gall bladder, pancreas, etc.) are all different – and more efficient – when a cat is fed the diet she is so beautifully designed to thrive upon.

There's a veritable smorgasbord of material illustrating the overall health benefits of raw-feeding, from improved oral health to reduction or outright elimination of a multitude of diseases to improved coat quality, a drastic jump in energy and a nice reduction in stool quantity and odor.

All the reasons we feed our healthy cats a raw diet apply twice as strongly to a cat who is coping with some type of illness; she needs the foods that are going to provide her with the highest level of nutrition and energy for the least amount of work – for an obligate carnivore, that's animal-based meats, organs and bones. And cats' natural, inborn defenses against bacteria don't disappear just because their health is compromised, or when they become FIV+ or catch an upper respiratory infection – the glands in their mouths still produce lysozyme-containing saliva, their stomach acids still kill incoming pathogens, their digestive tracts are still just about the shortest, comparatively-speaking, in the animal kingdom.

Why isn't this more widely known, or accepted? Why do so many raw-feeding experts and advocates tamp down the rhetoric when the discussion turns to sick cats? It is my belief that proponents begin waffling and throwing out caveats because we have all – every last one of us – been sold so solidly on the dangers of raw foods, especially meat(see *Let Em Eat Steak* for the history of meat-hate), that even in the face of plain logic, those doing the recommending can't stand their ground because they don't know – as in, don't have anything they can point to as proof (notwithstanding the thousands of years of evolution and wild living) – that raw feeding health-compromised cats is safe.

If something went wrong – even if it was completely unrelated to raw feeding – without that "real proof" of safety (i.e. scientific studies done on health-compromised animals), the cat's owner will be unable to know for sure he/she didn't hurt their furchild, and of course, no one wants to feel responsible for the pain of a cat that suddenly dies(so many pets have died from commercial pet food which was only sometimes later recalled, but who's counting?).

Logic and evolution, however, shouldn't be discounted simply because science hasn't gotten around to "proving" them. I believe it's both safe and the best choice we could make to feed health-compromised cats a raw diet. Right down to my bones, I believe that this is what cats ought to eat.

For those who want to start raw feeding their cats, but are having a difficult time with the concept, I offer you two viable compromises. If your preference is home-prepared, first rinse and then lightly sear the outside of the bone-less meats(never feed your cat cooked bone meats!) and organs you wish to feed (bacterial pathogens are nearly always on the outside of meats), and supplement with freeze dried bone or eggshell instead of real bones; once your cat returns to full health and / or you become comfortable with the raw-feeding concept, you can upgrade to a wholly fresh, raw diet with real bones.

If your preference is commercially-prepared foods, there is at least one – Nature's Variety – that guarantees their products are pathogen-free. Note: NV has a relatively high bone content and can cause some cats to become constipated, so it's best to feed in combination with plain meat meals.

In addition, for cats that have had to cope with a lifetime of overly processed kibble and canned foods and now have IBD or other digestive issues, you can purchase probiotics and digestive enzymes and sprinkle those over the raw foods, as per the directions, for a few weeks to help kick-start their digestive systems. Bottom line, not only are raw foods safe for our beloved felines, they are the highest in bio-available nutrition and the best foods you could feed, especially to health-compromised and FIV+ cats. Options are available for assuaging fears if needed, but what's important is to get the cat on a healthy species appropriate diet.

CHAPTER SEVEN

Dem Bones, 'Dem Bones, 'Dem... Scary Bones

Commercial or home-prepared, canned or raw, all balanced feline diets must contain whole bone or a substitute supplement. Unfortunately, the pet food industry began a highly successful campaign of misinformation in the 1980's that was critical of feeding "people food" in general and bones in particular. Today, just the thought of bones makes pet owners shudder, and many neophyte raw feeders shy away from offering bone-in meals to their beloved kitties for fear of harming them. Boneless meats are more expensive, so unless you spend time deboning them yourself, raw meat diets with only boneless meats are unbalanced by themselves and tend to get more expensive; you'll still need to add a supplement for the lack of bones in their meals. Bones are not just for Calcium as you will soon find out. Supplements are a poor substitute for the real thing, however, and every effort should be made to overcome these fears and allow cats the full natural expression of their carnivorous natures.

Why is whole raw meaty bone important?

Nutrients

Bone is composed of a handful of elements, but about 65 to 70 percent is comprised of the minerals Calcium and Phosphorus, which together form a calcium phosphate microcrystalline structure. Collagen, a fibrous protein, and small amounts of Chondroitin Sulfate, Keratin Sulfate and Phospholipids, make up the remaining 30 to 35 percent.

Calcium and Phosphorus are critical for the health of a cat's bones and teeth. Of all the minerals, however, Calcium is required in the greatest amount, especially in growing kittens. In addition to bones and teeth, it is essential for many functions including blood clotting, muscle contraction – such as the heart's pumping – and strength, and nerve impulse transmission. In addition, Calcium is used to help blood vessels move blood and to release hormones and enzymes that affect almost every function in the body. Nursing females need it to produce sufficient levels of milk.

Phosphorus is also very important, but is found in fairly high concentrations in meat. Phosphorus deficiencies are rarely noted in cats offered high-protein diets.

Bone marrow is mostly a fat and blood mixture full of amino acids and other high quality nutrients, and the cartilage that clings to bone is about 50% collagen. **Collagen** is important for a number of bodily processes and is the main component of skin, ligaments and tendons. Adequate Collagen in the diet inhibits joint pain, improves skin elasticity and promotes quicker healing of bone fractures and skin wounds. Feeding these elements in their natural form is the most effective and easiest way to ensure optimal digestion and absorption of the full nutrient profile. And raw bone-in meals offer much more than just their basic nutrients.

Dental Health

Eating whole bone offers unparalleled oral health benefits. Dental disease is at near-epidemic levels in the feline population – it's estimated that more than 85% of cats over three years old are suffering from periodontal disease – and has far reaching health consequences. Toxins and bacteria from the mouth travel throughout the bloodstream, stressing the immune system and infecting other organs, especially the heart and kidneys. Dental disease contributes to other diseases that can be fatal. Teeth rot and cause intense pain that can go unnoticed for months, even years. Around 30 to 40 percent of healthy adult cats suffer from Feline Tooth Resorptive Lesions, sometimes referred to as FORLS, a painful condition in which the teeth are slowly destroyed from the outside in, and many others are inflicted with Feline Stomatitis, an autoimmune disorder that causes painful inflammation of the mouth and throat tissues

A diet that includes tearing, ripping and scissoring through raw meat, tendons and bones provides the necessary stimulation to keep the cat's mouth clean and healthy. The firm resistance of these foods increases the number, distribution, and tone of the capillaries in the gums, improving the metabolism and vitality of all of the supporting and surrounding structures of the cat's mouth. The scraping action of the bones, muscle meats and tendons keeps the teeth clean and prevents food build-up, gingivitis and periodontal disease. A diet that includes whole bone is the single most effective method for preventing dental disease, and can even reverse some damage and restore health to the oral cavity.

The alternative is brushing the cat's teeth daily, something most feline owners find stressful for the cat and hazardous to their owners!

Digestive and Mental Health

In addition to the near-irreplaceable oral health benefits, the very act of scissoring through raw meat and bone sets off a physiological chain reaction that releases a highly efficient combination of enzymes in the cat's digestive system and this, combined with the extended time required to finish the meal, promotes a better digestive process. The cat's meals are assimilated with more efficacy, as every bit of nutrition is absorbed from her food.

Finally, there is substantial anecdotal evidence this active engagement in the eating process has several psychological benefits to the cat, including the satisfaction inherent in successfully meeting mental and physical challenges – eating becomes work! Cats fed a diet of meat chunks and whole bone seem to be calmer and less prone to aggression, irritation and discontent.

Risks

No act in life is risk free, but offering your cat raw bone-in meals carries not much more risk of choking than offering her kibble. Raw bones are soft and pliable and it is unlikely a cat will choke on them. Cats evolved to eat animals, bones and all, and most of them instinctively know how to go about it. You will learn how to pick the right sized animal(and cuts) for your cat later.

Chicken ribs or other bone-in meals cut too small may occasionally get stuck to the roof of the cat's mouth or go down her throat sidewise, and inexperienced cats may try to swallow too-large a piece of bone-in meal. The former may cause panic until the cat can dislodge the food, and the latter will cause the cat to regurgitate what she unsuccessfully tried to swallow (after which, she'll usually re-eat the meal in more manageable bites). Both of these can be avoided by offering pieces that are too large to be swallowed in one gulp, forcing the cat to cut her food into perfectly bite sized and easily swallowable pieces.

You can virtually eliminate the chance of a chipped or broken tooth by feeding only thin and non-weight-bearing bones; think of the bones you would find in a mouse, bird or small rabbit. Think quail, chicken necks and wing pieces. A good rule of thumb for bone size or density: if you can't cut it with good kitchen shears, don't feed it to your cat. Of course, never, ever feed your cat cooked bones, as they are brittle and can cause serious damage when eaten.

Transitioning

A domestic cat's natural diet consists of about 5-7% whole bone – rodents are roughly 5 percent bone, birds are slightly less and rabbits run just under 10 percent – and most prey model raw diets recommend 5 – 10 percent edible bone.

Always leave meat on the bones! It's how those bones are packaged in the wild and how you should offer them to your cat. This will encourage her to eat the meal and facilitate the smooth movement of the food when she swallows.

To transition, start with very small bones, like the ribs and wings from a hen/chicken or half a quail (note – small bones, not small bites!). Cats fed commercial products all their lives need to learn how to use their jaws and teeth to scissor through meat and bones, and they have to build up their jaw strength to be able to do so. They also get discouraged fairly easily, so you want to start with the easiest bone-in meals you can offer.

Transition slowly, over a few weeks, to give the cat's digestive system time to readjust to working at peak efficiency. If your cat throws up bones or you find a bit of bone in the stool, slow the transition even further.

Once your cat is familiar and comfortable with Cornish Hen and quail-sized bones, you can move up to chicken ribs, wings and legs(drumstick) . Estimating how much bone each cat needs can be difficult, but a good rule of thumb is offering three bone-in meals a week (assuming you're feeding three meals a day). Half the edible bone on a chicken breast with ribs, or the tip and two middle bones of a chicken wing (the "wingette") both make suitably-sized bone-in meals for most cats. You can use that as your starting point and adjust from there.

Determine how much adjusting you need to do by watching your cat's litter box. Firm but moist stools are perfect. Stools that are hard typically require a bit less bone in the diet and those that are loose require more; try not to exceed 10% however, as excessive amounts of bone can cause constipation.

Some kitties take to raw like they've been waiting all their lives for it!

Conclusion

The importance of raw bone-in meals is clear. Their nutrients are critical to good health and provided in the perfect combination and form for maximum utilization. The flossing and cleaning of the teeth and gums promotes dental health and supports the immune system, and a clean, bacteria- and toxin-free mouth minimizes stress upon the cat's organs. The evidence for digestive and mental health benefits is compelling, and there is minimal risk involved in offering appropriately-sized bone-in meals. Raw bones are neither dangerous nor scary, so why not let your kitty release her inner tiger by ripping into a real meat and bones meal tonight?

Excuse #1: "But I don't have the space to feed a fresh diet!"

I hear that a lot in the reasons why people who want to feed a fresh diet stick to feeding strictly commercial processed diets. Absolutely, if you have the space, you can definitely use it up easily doing a fresh or raw food diet by preparing larger batches of food for the freezer, shopping in bulk, ordering supplies online, getting meat from wholesalers, or from friends clearing out their freezers, and such. Some raw feeders even have entire freezers or multiple freezers for their cats and/or dogs, full of options to last months and months. And, yes, being able to do it that way can help keep costs down, but, not having that space doesn't have to hold you back; it just means doing things a little differently.

I share a home and have limited space: a bar fridge in a private area for our fresh produce, a shelf in the communal freezer, a cupboard for the dogs dry goods and dishes, a small box in the shared fridge of "on the go" foods for the dogs. I decided lack of space was not going to be a deterrent to me feeding the way I wanted to feed my cats.

It means shopping more regularly and not often anything in bulk. I shop for meat and raw dog food every 2 weeks. I shop for fresh 1-2 times a week, and, before it spoils, I freeze the fresh we didn't quite get to finish on time. I prepare the food by meal, by day, or by a few days at most. Not in batches that will last for weeks or months and need freezer space.

But, doesn't that take more time: shopping so often, starting from scratch all the time?

No. I suspect about the same time as it takes people to prepare big batches of dog food for the freezer. Sure, more than just scooping kibble into a bowl or opening a can but some things in life are just worth finding the time: especially because that may give you more time together with your cat in the long run.

Here are some photos:

Almond
Flour
Produce

Topmost : A fridge box with stuff that's up next.

Bottom Left: A cupboard where I can see at a glance what I've got and what I need (eg: need to get some sardines today), along with glass bowls, plates, and their dog bowls (in the washer right now).

Bottom Right: The freezer has a bin for produce type items, meat and fish, some almond and coconut flour and ground flax tucked in the back. There's always a package of green tripe on the go and ground chicken backs, and we're rotating through turkey, lamb, and goat in whole prey raw patties. I buy their patties in meats I don't usually eat myself and they get DIY meals out of meats we both eat such as chicken, beef, mutton, and rabbit.

Don't let space hold you back; you'll be surprised what you can do even if you don't have any!

"Well, ok, but my cats are doing fine on kibble and/or canned foods."

All cats look "fine," until they don't. I submit that most, if not all, kibble and canned fed cats are not feeling as well as they could; they are not truly ***thriving***. Cats are particularly good at hiding when they aren't feeling well, and their reputation for being lay-abouts works against them in this respect. I have been working with cat owners transitioning their cats to raw diets for a while now and the one most remarked upon change is always the extraordinary leap in energy and vitality their cats exhibit when fed a properly balanced raw diet. (Improved coat quality, sociability, general oral health and breath odor, and a large reduction in stool quantity and odor are also regularly seen improvements.)

The pet food industry serves, in large part, as the dumping ground for human food and agricultural industries. Dead, diseased, dying, disabled and drugged animals are fodder for the rendering vats, as are barrels of restaurant grease and food waste and truck loads of expired products from grocery stores (styrofoam packaging and all). Pet food products containing "meat meal," "meat and bone meal," and "poultry meal" are very likely to contain less-than-optimally nutritious and edible ingredients common pet owners would find very objectionable, were they aware.

Kibble and canned products are cooked down to the point of being virtually nutritionally inert. Additives are mixed in to give the foods flavor, texture and form, and to prevent spoilage. Foods that have no business in an obligate carnivore's diet are added for a variety of reasons unrelated to the cat's health, including profit and marketing effect. A mix of vitamins and minerals is added to give the food some nutritional value – a mix that is inherently incomplete because science has not yet identified all the nutrients cats get from their prey, nor in what combinations those nutrients are utilized by the cat's body. Quality control can be iffy and recalls, sometimes involving deaths, happen every few years for a myriad of reasons, including chemical contaminants, unhealthy or poisonous additives, and unbalanced vitamin / mineral mixes (mixes which are different for every manufacturer).

Kibble is a singularly inappropriate "food" product for cats. Because of the very nature of their manufacture, kibble requires some form of carbohydrate content. Many of them are loaded with grains, while others have substituted potatoes or another starch – seemingly benign, but in reality still a food the cat's body is ill-equipped to process.

Worst of all, being forced to process such a foreign diet stresses the cat's body enormously. That, combined with a chronically dehydrated state of being – as desert animal descendants, cats have a low thirst drive and an inefficient method of drinking water (their lapping mechanics are not the same as a dog's or as efficient) – and kibble is potentially the single largest underlying cause of many of the diseases and other illnesses sweeping in epidemic proportions across our domestic cat populations. Obesity, diabetes, urinary tract issues, inflammatory bowel disease (often a precursor for intestinal cancer, or lymphoma), kidney disease, allergies, vomiting and diarrhea are just a few of the ailments that have been linked in some manner to kibble-laden diets.

As Dr. Elizabeth Hodgkins, author of YourDiabeticCat.com, says in her book, *Your Cat: Simple New Secrets to a Longer, Stronger Life*, "I have never seen a single case of serious obesity, diabetes, urinary tract disease, or IBD in a cat fed meat instead of commercial dry foods. Many other people have seen the same results. Further, I do not see nutritional deficiencies in cats fed properly balanced raw-meat diets. I want to emphasize a point here. The incidence of these problems has not just declined on a raw-meat diet, they have entirely disappeared. These results are too dramatic to ignore."

Either because they are nutritionally deficient, because the additives are harmful in some manner, or a combination of both, even cats being fed what most regard as the healthiest of canned food products exhibit unmistakable signs of improved vitality and health when transitioned to a balanced raw diet.

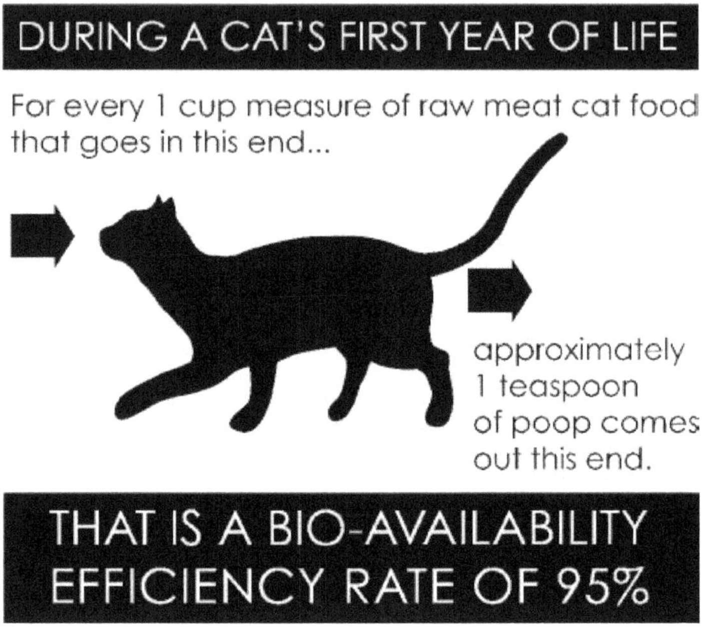

Credits: The Raw Meat Cat Food Cookbook What Your Cat Wants to Eat Whether They Know It or Not (Holly Ollivander Huw Thomas)

CHAPTER EIGHT

RAW FEEDING YOUR HOUSE-CAT: WHAT'S ALL THE FUSS ABOUT?

Since the 2007 pet food poisoning that killed over 8,500 cats and dogs and resulted in a massive pet food recall, pet owners have been looking more closely at what they feed their beloved cats and dogs. Websites have sprung up discussing the topic in great detail; some written by veterinarians, many by individuals who lost pets from contaminated foods in 2007 and since. One of the diets receiving increasing scrutiny and fast-growing support is raw feeding. Advocates are, in some cases, nearly rabid(excuse my pun) in their praise and defense of the various raw-feeding methods.

Why is this one diet receiving so much attention?

It's what the cat is uniquely, specifically, beautifully designed to eat. Proper nutrition is the building block upon which a body's health is built, and this applies doubly so to obligate carnivores, whose dietary needs are very sharply defined. Like birds of prey, snakes and sharks, cats are designed inside and out to catch and eat whole prey. Every aspect of the cat's physiology demonstrates that obtaining what it needs to achieve optimum health – not just survive but truly thrive – depends upon fulfilling its fresh, prey-based dietary requirements.

Raw feeding your house-cat: What's all the fuss about? From their sharp eyesight, keen hearing and fearsome claws and teeth, to their exceptional stalking, pouncing and sprinting abilities, the cat's body is built to hunt. Apex predators are present in nearly every environment they occupy, they are one of nature's most perfectly designed killing machines. The Dragonfly and Praying Mantis, both a favorite for my cats, are two lesser known examples of apex predators. Ah! the circle of life.

Cats are so well designed, in fact, there has been virtually no genetic drift in the 10,000 years since the African Wild Cat ancestors of today's house-cats were brought out of the Middle Eastern deserts. That tabby purring so contentedly on your lap is virtually indistinguishable, at the genetic level, from today's African Wild Cat.As efficient a predator as they are outwardly, the cats' digestive physiology is even more specialized around their prey-based dietary needs.

Starting at the very basic digestive level, a meal that includes large amounts of animal protein causes an increased flow of saliva, as well as production of the most effective combination of digestive enzymes in that saliva. Similarly, the stomach, gall bladder, pancreas, and upper and lower intestines all secrete a mix of enzymes that are positively responsive to the presence of large amounts of animal protein, ensuring a high level of digestive efficacy throughout the entire digestive tract. Animal tissues, bones and organs are chemically broken down and assimilated at an extremely high level of efficiency and thoroughness, providing the cat with maximal nutrients while expending minimal energy. Cats fed standard commercial diets must expend more energy to digest their foods more thoroughly, and do not enjoy the smaller, less smellier and less frequent stools of raw-fed cats. More importantly, cats metabolize animal protein and fat directly for their energy. Protein is used for daily body repair and building as well as energy, and calories from protein are either used or excreted. Comparatively-speaking, cats require a fairly high level of fat in their diet – about 20% – and that, too, is thoroughly and efficiently utilized. You will seldom encounter an overweight cat on a balanced raw diet.

Conversely, cats have no dietary need for carbohydrates and have actually lost some of the enzymatic pathways needed to process them; since there is no pathway for energy conversion, carbs are processed and stored as fat. A carb-heavy diet will stress the cat's digestive system and reduce the efficiency of protein absorption. If the diet does not contain enough animal protein for their daily needs, or they are unable to process an adequate amount of that protein, cats will sabotage the muscles of their own bodies to obtain their daily needs. Additionally, feline satiety is signaled by the ingestion of sufficient amounts of animal protein in their food; lacking it, they will be always hungry/ asking for food and consistently overeat, resulting in yet more carbs being converted to fat.

Furthermore, because the following nutrients are found so abundantly in the bodies of their prey, cats – unlike most animals – are unable to synthesize them and must get their daily requirements from their diet:

• Eleven different amino acids: arginine, histidine, isoleucine, leucine, lysine, methionine, phenylalanine, threonine, tyrptophan, valine, and, of course, taurine.
• Vitamins A and D.
• Niacin. (Although cats can create this to some degree, the amount is insufficient to their needs and they must consume it daily.)
• The fatty acid Arachadonic Acid(AA).

There is an intimate relationship between the cat's natural diet and the animal's intestinal characteristics, and what a cat eats affects how that food is digested. From the greater amount and more efficient composition of saliva secreted during the meal to the increased activity of stomach and intestinal enzymes and other digestive secretions to the increased speed at which food is moved through the digestive tract, high animal-protein/high moisture diets have a health-promoting effect. Eating such a diet is not only good for the cat from a nutritional perspective – it causes a chain reaction of chemical events that actively increases the cat's ability to pull maximum nutrition from the food while bolstering the animal's natural defenses against internal and external pathogens.

Conclusion

Evolution, science and logic all point to a fresh raw prey-based diet as being the most appropriate, nutritious, and easily-digestible diet for today's cats, and the anecdotal evidence is overwhelmingly in favor of raw diets. With the increased scrutiny being given to what pet owners feed their littlest family members, it's easy to foresee a time when they will consider feeding raw products to cats and dogs as common-sense healthy as we do giving whole, fresh foods to our kids. Not everyone eats or serves whole apples in a fast-food Apple Danish, but there is no doubt in our minds which of the two is healthier.

Raw Feeding 101

There are three ways to feed a raw diet – commercial raw food(which is usually frozen or dried), homemade Prey Model Raw(PMR) and Prey Model Raw Whole(PMR Whole) – and each has pros and cons. Commercial Raw foods are convenient and typically no more expensive than premium cat manufactured wet food diets.(See Sources & Resources section for online sellers in India selling Raw Cat Food).

P.S: I haven't tried commercial options in India so I cannot vouch for them. I have no affiliations with any of the companies listed as recommendations. These are recommendations only; the only reason I've listed them is because there are not a lot of commercial raw options in India at the time of compiling the book.

Homemade diets require a bit more preparation, but are typically less expensive than the other options and provide complete control over ingredient mix and quality. Whole Prey Model Raw(PMR) provides the highest nutritional profile possible, is usually the most expensive, this method is by far the easiest to prep and feed (just thaw the whole prey and serve!). We will not be exploring Whole PMR in this book. See Resources for more info about feeding this way.

Transitioning Your Cat to Raw

The questions I receive the most are all related to transitioning a cat to raw. They are also sometimes the most difficult to answer, as there are many variables. What is the cat eating now? What kind of raw diet are you interested in? How flexible is your cat? What products can you source? And more. I've arranged the information in the order I think would be the easiest to assimilate. Giving our beloved cats the gift of species-appropriate nutrition is the single most important act of love a cat owner can engage in; I hope this information makes that gift an easier one to deliver!

Keep these three things in mind as you transition your cat to raw.

Since its appearance in the US in the 1930's, the pet food industry has been extraordinarily successful in its marketing campaigns, convincing an entire generation they are inherently incapable of feeding their pets without "expert" guidance and erasing over 10,000 years of evolutionary fact; cats are obligate carnivores that thrive on a raw, prey-based diet. Humans have been feeding cats ever since we domesticated them long before these pet food companies came along. Today, feeding raw meat, bones and organs to our beloved pets is considered a novel and dangerous concept.

The truth is, of course, that cats don't just thrive on such a diet, they have a physiological need for it. Furthermore, there are raw commercial products available that meet the same AAFCO guidelines (if it is your gold standard) as balanced homemade products, and anyone willing to put a little thought and time into it can create a relatively inexpensive and balanced diet right in the convenience of their own homes.

Raw is what cats are designed to eat, and feeding it can be both easy and economically feasible.

Once you decide how to source your cat's new diet, your next step is convincing him that he prefers it over his current food. Although each type of diet – ground, prey model and whole prey – has its own transition tricks, these guidelines apply to any transition and will go a long way toward ensuring your efforts are successful.

To summarise, apart from commercial raw cat food there are three main types of Raw Food diets for Cats:
1.Prey Model Raw(PMR) Ground
2. Prey Model Raw(PMR) Whole
3. Whole Prey Model.

We will explore the first two in this book.

Don't Stress It.

First and foremost, don't stress the transition. You are not in a race and unless your cat is suffering ill effects on his current diet, there is no reason to rush, nor is there is there a time limit. This is a lifestyle change for you both that might involve starts and stops and perhaps even a has little backpedaling. It might seem like you are taking two steps ahead and one step back. There's nothing wrong with that! However long it takes, however slow and convoluted your progress may become, don't push, don't hover, and don't stress. Patience is a virtue.

Cats are sensitive creatures and pick up emotions easily. If you are hovering over him, shedding anxiety and begging him to just eat one bite (and I have counseled owners who have done exactly this). Your cat is more likely to want to hide from whatever is happening and this will make you so upset than he will refuse to eat. It's a vicious cycle.

So relax. Take it easy, and enjoy each milestone as your cat learns to eat the way nature intended for him. You will be better able to manage and even enjoy his progress. I have spoken with many owners who exclaimed that despite cringing during the first few bone-in meals, the sound of their cats chomping through bone now gives them a curious sense of satisfaction; and so it will be with you.

Let your cat set the pace.

Many owners are so excited when they first learn of the benefits of raw feeding, or so appalled when they come to understand the true nature of standard commercial diets, they want their cats switched to raw overnight. This can happen, but it's rare (except for kittens) and if you push your cat too hard, you'll sabotage your own efforts.

Cats, just like people, have difference personalities and preferences. Whatever your cat's unique perspective, allow him to take the transition at his pace. Kittens and some adventurous cats and willing to dive right into a new food. They may take to raw in a single meal! Others are more timid and need to see and smell the new food several times before venturing a bite. Many, unfortunately, are addicted to kibble and are initially reluctant to even try anything new. Every cat is different, and every transition unique.

You may also encounter this situation I encountered with my 8 year old male cat Tubby - he ate his raw meals(two a day, with a small one in between or before bed) for a week really well and then suddenly seemed disinterested in food. I got disheartened after two days of leaving the meat to thaw for him and feeding his thawed food to my eager dogs. He didn't eat for two whole days and on the third morning he ate a full packet of whiskas wet food(I always keep some commercial wet cat food pouches in case of emergencies!).That's when I knew his appetite is back and thawed his food to serve him. My theory is that because Raw food is so much more superior to what he used to eat, his body was doing a little detox. Or he was just being a brat!

In addition to preferences, cats need to learn how to scissor through meat, skin, tendon and, eventually, small bones, and they need to work up the jaw strength to do so. They are easily discouraged, so it's important to start small and slow, setting the cat up to be successful at every step. A cat that attempts to crunch through a thigh bone (which is too thick for most cats) and fails will often be reluctant to make another attempt at a bone-in meal, even when offered something as easy to break down such as quail ribs. I hold chicken drumsticks in my hand for Tubby eat. If your cat is lifelong kibble eater, start with boneless meats or organs. Chop them up.

Never try to force your cat to eat the new food. And never try to starve him into eating it, as you could cause him to become very ill within a remarkably short time. Cats are prone to a serious and potentially fatal disease called hepatic lipidosis, or "fatty liver disease" that is brought on by starvation. It can happen in as little as 48 hours, especially if they are overweight, so don't let your cat skip more than a couple of meals. Offer him whatever it takes to get him eating regularly again and then start the transition over at the point just before he began refusing food. Moving at the cat's pace will ensure he feels confident and comfortable as you move forward with the new diet.

Serve three or four scheduled meals.

One of the biggest hurdles to a successful transition is the all-you-can-eat kibble buffet served in so many feline homes. There is very little incentive for a cat that is never truly hungry to try something new.

If you're free-feeding, your first transition step is to accustom your cat to scheduled meals. This may mean starting with several small meals a day, but the goal is to work it down to three (or four, if you can manage it).

If you're not free-feeding, but only offering one or two meals, your first transition step will make your cat very happy – you will need to add that second or third meal.

Most cat owners are unaware that meal frequency impacts their cats' health, and there is a lot of confusion around how often a domesticated cat should be fed. The majority are either free-fed or fed only once or twice a day, despite the fact cats evolved to spend most of their time hunting and would naturally eat between 8 – 12 small meals every 24 hours. Because it's so important, I'm going to digress and summarize why offering at least three or four meals to adult cats (and four or five meals to kittens) is strongly recommended.

First, smelling food triggers a cat's digestive system to begin working, and constantly smelling food – as free-fed cats do – keeps that system primed and ready to go all day, pulling energy from other systems and, potentially causing issues like premature aging, poor coat quality, and chronic cystitis. In addition, a carnivore's digestive physiology has incorporated hunger as an integral part of its healthy workings. Indigestible solids are retained in the stomach until digestion of other food products is completed and it is, in fact, hunger pangs is what propels this material forth. If the cat is never allowed to become hungry, the regulation of waste movement is compromised, leading to discomfort, hairball regurgitation and other digestive issues.

On the flip side, the cat's stomach can't expand like the dog's to accommodate large meals, and cats can – and often do – regurgitate if fed too much at one time, as might happen with a cat fed only once or twice daily. Eating too fast, as cats tend to do when they are very hungry, can also cause discomfort and regurgitation of the meal. Additionally, as the cat becomes hungry, the buildup of bile acids in the stomach can cause him to become nauseous, provoking what many have termed "hunger pukes."

Finally, the frequency of a cat's meals impacts the pH of his urine. 'Post-prandial alkaline tide' refers to the increase in urine alkalinity that follows the ingestion of a large meal, a pH change that can lead to the formation of painful and potentially deadly struvite crystals. Eating smaller, more frequent meals – mimicking their instinctive hunting behavior – naturally helps maintain a cat's pH in the normal range. It only makes sense that following the cat's evolutionary behavior patterns as closely as possible will provide the most benefits to the cat, and offering at least three or four meals a day is a workable balance for most adult cats and their owners (before work, after work, and just before bed).

Be flexible, but persistent.

We all know how "finicky" cats can be, how often they change their finicky little minds. During the transition, you'll likely encounter days when your cat refuses something he ate with gusto the day before. Don't let this discourage you. Keep offering different meats or meals. Use briberies liberally (sprinkles of freeze-dried chicken treats, etc.) on top of the food you're offering, but don't be afraid to take a step back to the last thing he ate, even if it means offering smaller meat chunks or less raw mixed with some canned.

Some cats(especially kittens) will take to raw after a single meal; others may take weeks or months. Kibble addicts often take several weeks. Some might run into problems with certain products or meats, such as constipation related to bone-heavy commercial blends, or intolerance to grain-fed beef and chicken meats. Take care while feeding novel meats like turkey, as the necks are much bigger and can be a chocking hazard for older, inexperienced-in-meat-eating cats. Turkey necks are much bigger than chicken necks. Hammer them and they are safe to eat. Always supervise your cat when they are eating bones; especially older kibble-fed 10+ year old cats that lack enough jaw strength to cut through bony meat and eat meat. Kibble-fed cats also try to eat meat hastily just like they ate their kibble. Knowing the heimlich maneuver for cats is a useful skill to have in case of a choking emergency. A few cats may do fine for several weeks after a full transition, only to suddenly run into an issue that causes you to back-pedal a bit.

Don't let any of these delays, plateaus or problems discourage you. And above all, don't let a troublemaker cat make you give up. No matter how long it takes to get your feline friend to accept a raw diet, you can outwait him. Your persistence and patience will pay off in an immeasurably healthier, longer-lived and happier feline companion.

Conclusion

Although the ease and timeframe may differ, all cats can be transitioned to raw; just research and learn what tricks and tips work best with your chosen diet and combine them with the four basic tactics described here. Thousands of cat owners have already done it – and seen their cats' health make amazing improvements – and you can too!

Transition Guide: Making the switch to ground raw.

Although it's difficult to answer generic raw feeding transition questions due to the variables unique to each cat owner's situation, and pretty much impossible to create a precise "1-2-3 Steps to Transition" that will work for every cat, I can, however, offer a guideline loaded with tips that can be adapted to your particular circumstances.

Take a chance!

First thing? Go ahead and offer your cat a plate of ground raw. If she takes it, then you're good to go and can begin feeding raw right away. Many cats need a gradual transition, but some take to raw like they've been waiting all their lives for it! Give your kitty the chance to dive right in! This is especially true for younger cats. Young cats and kittens haven't yet had their "tastes" distorted by canned or kibble product textures and (overly pungent) odors and often take to raw foods quite readily.

Note: If possible, kittens should be weaned directly to prey model or whole prey meals so they don't have to re-learn how to eat later when you're ready to upgrade from ground raw. If your cat doesn't accept the raw right away, then you can move into your transitioning plan.

Ease your way into it.

At this point, you've already accustomed your cat to eating 3 - 4 scheduled meals a day and you should, of course, be feeding her on a flat plate (to respect those delicate whiskers). This is critical – if you do not close the 24/7 kibble buffet before you start transitioning your kitty to raw, you will be undermining all of your efforts to get her on a healthy diet and setting you and your kitty up to fail.

To begin the transition, roll the ground raw meat into a pea-sized ball and put it on the side of the plate next to your cat's regular food, then put her plate down. Leave the plate down for 30 minutes to give her a chance to try the raw out of curiosity – then take it up and throw it away(or feed it to a stray!). Even if she ignores the raw completely, having it there will acquaint her with the sight and smell of it, and over time, she will begin to associate it with food.

Buy or make several different batches of the raw and rotate through them just as you do (or should be doing) with her regular meals.

You can also just mix the ground raw right into your cat's regular canned or kibble food, but you'll need to be watchful with this method. Some cats will eat around the raw if they can, and some will refuse to eat the mixed food altogether.

Skipping one or two meals a week shouldn't cause any issues, but missing too many meals – especially if your cat is overweight – can cause hepatic lipidosis, a life-threatening disease. So you can't use hunger to force your cat to eat something new, and you shouldn't let her skip multiple meals or go more than a day without eating. If she won't eat the mixed food over one or two meals, either give her what she will eat and offer the raw on the side, or offer both the regular food and some mixed food at every meal.

Transitioning your cat should be a relaxed affair for both of you, not an ordeal.

Note: It's a good idea to weigh your cat weekly during the transition to be sure she isn't losing too much weight, or losing weight too quickly. Any loss exceeding 1-2% of her body weight per week is too much!

After a few days to a week, most cats will be eating the little balls of raw, whether separately or mixed in. If your cat is not, however, don't despair. Just accept that you'll be throwing some food away and keep patiently offering it to her. The longest I've personally seen a cat ignore that dollop of raw food was 29 days, but I've read accounts of longer periods. The key here is patience: however long it takes for her to try that first bite is however long it takes.

Once she's eating that one pea-size ball of raw regularly for a few days, add another pea-sized ball. A few days after she's eating both of those at most meals, add a third. Start reducing the regular food while you continue to slowly increase the amount of raw until you are feeding all raw. Remember not to pressure the cat. Switch at her pace, and if she starts balking at the amount of new food just back up a step or two. A little back and forth is to be expected, so don't let it get you down.

Even cats that readily gulp down raw the first time it's offered will sometimes refuse it later. This is part of the transition process! Just take a step back in the transition, hold steady for a few meals, and then continue on with the transition. A relaxed and patient approach is critical to a successful transition, but there are many ways to help support and speed up the process.

Tips and tricks to support the transition.

Here's a list of things you can do to encourage your kitty to accept her new and improved menu:

Draw out your cat's hunting instinct by engaging her in interactive play sessions with fishing pole-type toys for a few minutes, ending the play by allowing her to "catch the prey" and then replacing the toy with her food. This will stimulate her appetite and prime her for eating. (As an added benefit, interactive play improves the bond between the two of you and reduces feline stress levels.)

Many cats don't care for cold food, so take the chill off by mixing in a teaspoon of warm water or putting it in a plastic bag and floating it in a bowl of warm water for 10 minutes or so. Think mouse body temperature! (Don't microwave her raw food – you'll destroy some of the delicate nutrients that make fresh foods so healthy in the first place.)

Using the tips of your fingers and your nails, stroke your cat around her neck and shoulders and down her back while she's in front of the food bowl. Some cats will be stimulated to eat when petted like this.

Bribe your kitty into eating by sprinkling enticements over the new food. Some proven options to try: catnip, grated Parmesan Cheese, Forti Flora flakes, fish food flakes, her favorite wet cat food, fish flakes, or crumbled up freeze-dried or dehydrated meat treats. You can also drip a bit of water-packed canned tuna juice or squeeze creamy treats over it, but be careful to drip/sprinkle as minimally as possible and wean the kitty off as soon as possible – both are unhealthy in anything but small amounts and are quite addictive.

The best method to transition from canned/kibble to raw is to not mix it in with the raw, instead you can drip the canned food juice or sprinkle a little crushed kibble over it.

Note: During this transition, keep kibble products as closed up as possible, preferably in the refrigerator or even outside the house if you can. Cats have an incredible sense of smell and if she can smell it, she may be tempted to hold out for it. As soon as you can, get rid of it completely.

Feed your kitty some of the raw off your fingertip. Some cats will take from our hands what they won't initially try on their own.

If it doesn't upset your cat, squish a bit of the raw onto her paw and let her lick it off.

Offer your cat a piece of lightly cooked chicken, beef, pork, etc., or some garlic-free baby food (meat-based). If she likes it, add it to the ground raw/canned mix.

Crate your cat for meals! Skittish cats and cats in multi-cat homes will often feel more secure and relaxed in a crate, making them more willing to try new foods. You have an added benefit here in that when you switch to the whole meat meals of prey model, your cat will already be accustomed to eating in a crate and will not be able to drag the meat chunks all over your house.

Conclusion: Have patience!

I know I've said it before, but your most important resource for transitioning your cat is going to be your patience. All cats can be switched to a healthier diet, given enough time. Don't let setbacks discourage you. Expect them, roll with them, and then slowly get back on your transition plan. You're not in a race, this is a lifestyle change for both of you and your goal is to make it happen, not to make it happen in a specific timeframe.

If you need help maintaining a positive outlook, join one of the friendlier raw feeding groups for support. CatCentric has a Facebook group with amazingly supportive members who specialize in helping cat owners make this transition.

A few cats will accept raw immediately while others may take several weeks for a full transition. Most cats, however, will fall somewhere in between. Proper nutrition is critical to all aspects of feline health, so however long it takes for your cat, it is well worth the effort involved.

CHAPTER NINE

THE BASICS OF RAW FEEDING

When cat owners start researching feline nutrition, the amount of data they have to weed through can be overwhelming. And when they finally reach the conclusion that a wholesome, species-appropriate raw diet is what they should be feeding, they're only half way home.

There are several methods that can be used to raw feed cats, and there are an infinite number of opinions about which one is "right". In truth, any balanced raw diet will provide your cat with enormous nutritional benefits when compared to standard commercial diets. Which one you choose to feed should depend upon your particular resources, lifestyle and personal preferences, and not so much on someone else's opinion but your own.

Overview

Raw diets can be either bought pre-mixed, or made at home, and each method has its pros and cons. Commercially packaged raw foods are convenient and often no more expensive than standard commercial diets, but they are still commercially manufactured and run the same quality control risks as all processed products. They are also, at this time, available in ground mixes only. Home-made diets can be prepared in three forms – ground, prey model raw (PMR) and whole prey – ground prey model raw (PMR) require a bit more preparation and serving time(as the method suggests, you'll need a meat grinder for this). Home-made PMR diets, however, are typically the least expensive feeding option, home-preparing your cat's food allows you complete control over the ingredient mix and quality.

Whichever diet you chose, variety should be a key component. If you go with commercial, feeding several flavors from multiple manufactures will help prevent feline fixation on any one product – a problem if they change or stop producing it – and protect your cat from potential quality control issues by diluting the impact. In addition, since cats can develop hypersensitivity when continually exposed to the same proteins or ingredients for extended periods, rotating through several products will help prevent food intolerance issues.

If you're home-preparing your cat's diet, variety will be necessary to ensure she receives a complete nutritional profile. Studies have shown that lions and other big cats require 5 -7 different protein sources to fulfill their nutritional requirements, but it is generally accepted that 3 to 5 is sufficient for their domesticated cousins. Think Chicken, Beef, Mutton/Lamb, Rabbit, Turkey and Quail - these meats are available in most metros in India. Of course, providing more than five proteins can't do anything but improve the nutritional profile you're feeding. And don't forget insects! You can feed a handful of crickets every week (just drop them in the tub with the drain cover on) to add trace amounts of nutrients to your cat's diet while simultaneously allowing your miniature tiger to exercise some of her hunting instincts.

One caveat to sourcing a maximum variety of foods; keep fish products out of the rotation, as they are not a healthy addition in anything but small amounts. They can contribute to urinary tract issues due to their high magnesium content, and can cause both thiamine and Vitamin E deficiencies. Only one species in 22 eats only raw fish, so fish is not ideal as a predominant portion of a cat's diet. A single sardine once or twice a week, however, is a great source of Omega 3's and will avoid the problems associated with large amounts of other fish types.

Generally, you can feed your cat anywhere between 2% to 4% of her weight. More laid-back cats that don't get a lot of exercise and those with slow metabolisms can be fed at the lower end, energetic cats and those with fast metabolisms can be fed more frequently, for a minimum 2-3 times a day.

Commercial Raw Food

There are a large number of commercial raw products available today and more are coming to market all the time. In addition to an awareness of each manufacturer's quality control practices and history, you should carefully review the ingredients list of these products. Some contain fruits and vegetables which, though not needed in a cat's diet, it shouldn't cause any digestive issues if present at or less than 5%.

Pay attention to the meat/bone/organ percentages, as well. Some products contain more than 10% bone and amounts that high can cause constipation. These foods are fine to feed if included as part of a rotation of products from multiple manufacturers, but you should keep a careful eye on the litter box. Counter the high bone content by adding some boneless meat, raw organs and/or a quail whole egg/chicken egg yolk to the kitty bowl.

Other products contain no bone at all, and these can be included in a rotation of foods but very sparingly. Too little bone in a cat's diet will lead to loose stools and, over the long term, much more serious issues. These foods can't be fed as the sole diet without some type of bone supplement. Powdered eggshell is natural supplement for such meals; feeding Raw Meaty Bones thrice a week is sufficient for adult cats.

Speaking of which, synthetic supplements, too, can cause issues. Generally speaking, the more additives a raw food has, the more likely it is that something in the food may cause a digestive upset. Try to feed raw food and supplements with minimal to no fillers and preservatives with a natural origin.

Commercial raw products are currently only available in ground form. This is a benefit for many, as it is closer to the canned foods most commercial-fed cats have been eating and may be more acceptable to those cats than prey model or whole prey raw diets. Unfortunately, ground diets do not provide the dental and psychological benefits of PMR whole prey and many cats will eventually stop accepting ground in favor of something they can sink their teeth into.

Home-prepared Raw Food

Ground and prey model home-prepared diets are based on

a general guideline used by raw dog feeders for decades and slightly modified for the cats' smaller prey: the 83/7/5/5 rule; that's roughly 83% meat, fat, skin, sinew, connective tissue and heart, 7% edible bone, 5% liver, and 5% other secreting organ (kidney, thymus, spleen, pancreas, brain, eyes etc).

Whole prey, of course, is as close to natural as your cat can get without catching dinner on its own.

Whole Prey Meal with Mice and Eggs.Credits: @the_primalpack

A ground home-prepared raw diet involves grinding all the meats, organs, and bones together. It is convenient in its simplicity and offers the same cost savings of PMR, but like commercial diets, it does not provide a chewing challenge to the cat and, due to the nutrient breakdown inherent in the mechanical grinding process, typically requires supplementation. There are several tried and true ground diet recipes that can be found online, although it may take some research to find them. The Feline Nutrition Education Society's website and Dr. Lisa Pierson's website are good places to start.

In a prey model raw diet (also called a "frankenprey" diet), a variety of animal parts are fed in measured amounts so that over a certain period of time, usually a week, the cat will eat approximately the same sum of parts as it would have were it eating whole animals. Meals are often all meat or a mix of meat with bone or organ and are fed in large chunks that the cat must actively gnaw on to reduce to bite-size pieces that can be swallowed. This active engagement in the eating process has several benefits for the cat, including the psychological satisfaction inherent in successfully meeting mental and physical challenges (eating becomes work!). One of its more important benefits, however, is improved dental health. Dental disease is at near-epidemic levels in the feline population and has far-reaching health consequences for the cat. A diet that includes tearing, ripping and scissoring through meat, tendons and bones provides the necessary stimulation to keep your cat's mouth clean and healthy.

In addition, the very act of scissoring through chunks of fresh raw protein sets off a chain reaction that releases a more efficient combination of enzymes in the cat's digestive system (starting with the saliva) and this, combined with the extended time required to finish a meal, promotes an easier, more efficient digestive process.

Most of the meats, bones and organs for home-made ground and PMR diets can be bought in local grocery stores or online, making these diets fairly easy to source. Additional products, especially organs, can be found in meat stores or ordered online. Organic products are just as much healthier for your cat as they are for you, but are not critical to a balanced raw diet. Aim for human- grade meat and you're good.

Whole prey diets are the least common of the three home-prepared options. Although feeding whole animals such as mice, rats, young chicks, and quail is, obviously, the most natural method, it is the least acceptable to both cat owners, who sometimes find it emotionally difficult to handle small dead animals, and cats, who often have trouble even recognizing the prey as food. If both owner and cat can get past these difficulties, however, whole prey is the easiest, most nutritious and beneficial method of raw feeding. Animals for these diets can be purchased from local stores that cater to reptile owners or from a growing number of online vendors. Prey model raw(PMR) and whole prey diets generally require no supplementation, but, again, variety is key.

One thing to keep in mind with a PMR diet is the need for a schedule. Maintaining the 83/7/10 balance is critical, and if your daily schedule is anything like mine, writing down a weekly plan and taping it to the refrigerator will go a long way to ensuring you don't forget any important components.

Conclusion

You're almost guaranteed to encounter pushback when you decide to switch your kitty to a raw diet – especially from your allopathic veterinarian – and you're going to hear and read a wide range of sometimes conflicting opinions. Try not to stress it! A balanced species-appropriate diet is so extraordinarily nutritious it's really hard to go wrong, and one of the many cool aspects of raw feeding is that this diet – unlike canned or kibble – can be completely customized for your individual needs. Between commercial and home-prepared, raw feeders have an extensive array of selections to choose from, so no matter what your time, financial or logistical resources, there's a raw food option that will fit your lifestyle.

Time and Sanity Saving Tips

Storing Homemade Cat Food

Question: If I make my own cat food, what should I store it in?

Answer: Go for containers that hold just enough food that, once it's thawed, can be used up within a day or two – three days maximum. Personally, I like using pint-sized, sturdy, wide-mouth, glass or plastic freezer jars for storing the food. In my house at least, the pint size holds just the right amount of food (more or less) to feed two cats one day's worth of food.

The wide-mouthed version of these jars makes it super-easy and fast to portion the food into the jars on foodmaking day. The "can-or-freeze" variety of canning jars are good – protecting the food from freezer burn.

I've had the same jars for many, many years now and the only part I've periodically replaced are the metal lids that, over time, tend to get worn out.

Save yourself time and frustration by organizing supplies,

learning pro tips from those who have been doing this a long time, taking a little time to plan storage and serving, and walking the delicate line between patience and stubbornness in feeding a home-prepared diet to a fussy cat.

If you're going to make cat food for the long haul, making the process efficient (and playing your fave music while you're doing it) will increase chances you won't abandon the project.

Get Your Stuff Together

Keep all your dry ingredients together in ONE place in the kitchen, so you can easily find everything and not have to hunt it all down every time you make cat food.

Kitchen shears or a good tough pair of kitchen scissors can sometimes be easier than a knife for cutting and chunking the meats. Slightly frozen meat is easier to chop. Personally, I'm a klutz with my cleaver. But many experienced raw food makers swear by them. Good luck with that. I use inexpensive kitchen scissors.

For any of the ingredients that you can buy either in capsules or tablets, go for the capsules. If you start spending too much time on little things like crushing tablets in a mortar and pestle, there's a danger you'll give up making your own cat food. That would be terrible.

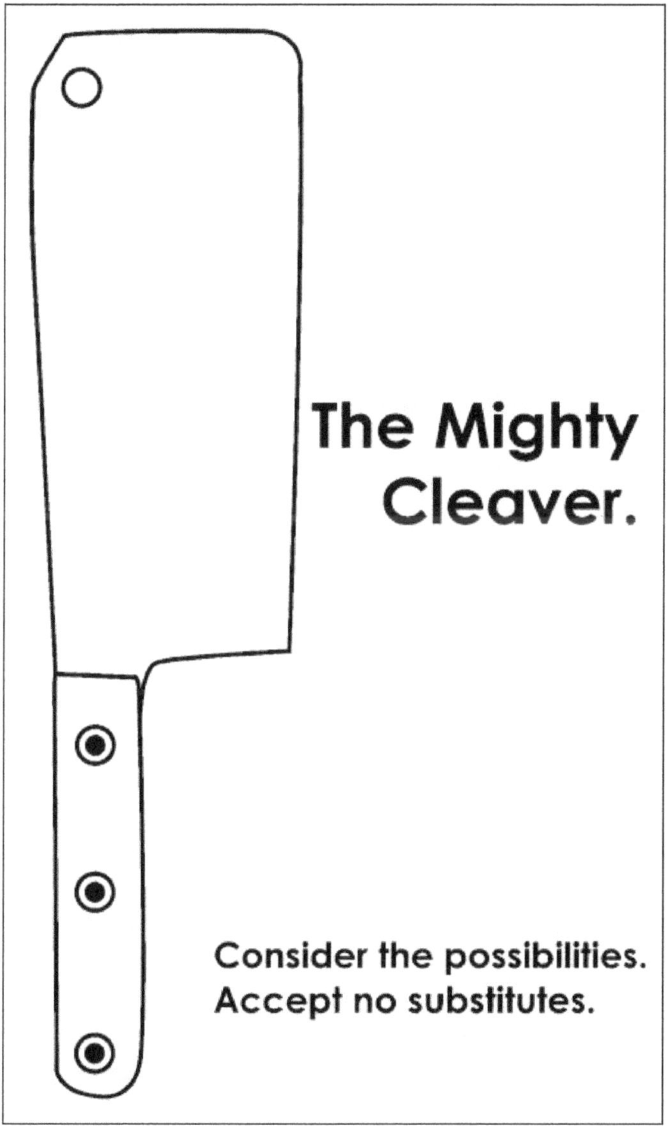

The Meat Cleaver/Meat Knife

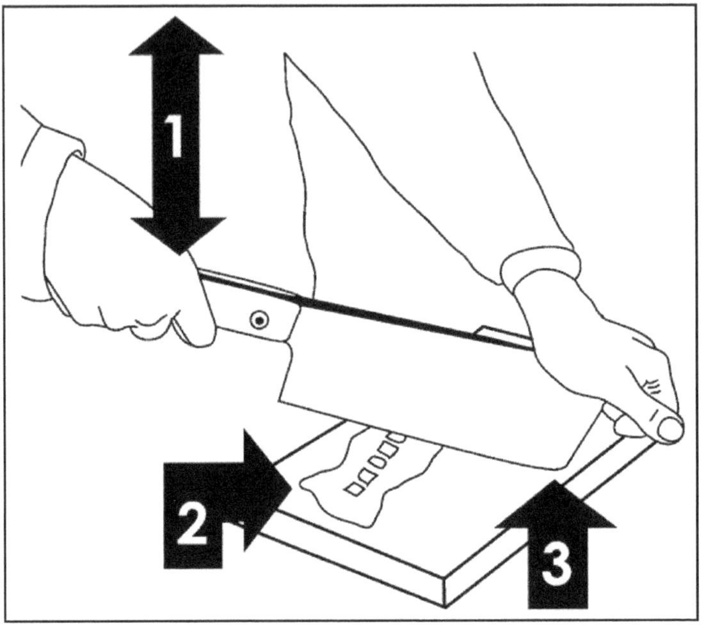

The right way to use a cleaver

Make Things Easier on Yourself

Buy the vitamin E in dry powder form in capsules. It's much easier to deal with than those little oil-filled capsules. Keep a little safety pin in the supplement compartment to pierce the capsules and empty them into the bowl.

If opening capsules is driving you nuts, you can simply put the capsules in some water (warmed up just a bit) and give them about 20 to 30 minutes to dissolve. Make sure they're completely dissolved and mixed in with all the water. You don't want kitty biting into a capsule and deciding she doesn't like the taste of raw food any more. If you're impatient or just want to speed things up, use an immersion blender to make the process faster.

Keep your knives sharp. Dull knives make the process last too long and can be more dangerous to use than sharp ones. Be smart and be careful: don't cut yourself. Cats need meat, yes, but not yours.

An egg separator can make things a little easier and faster too. Or just use your palm and fingers as the sieve to separate them.

Don't try and guess the weights of meats or organs — use a scale. You can get them cheaply on amazon or inexpensively at some stores; there's no need to buy a fancy, pricey one for cat food-making purposes.

That said, don't lose your mind about weights either. Inevitably, if you buy a chicken or rabbit, it's rarely going to weigh exactly the amount the recipe calls for. You may need to adjust a bit and add more or less water and adjust the supplements accordingly. But don't get your undies all in a bundle over this. Cats in the wild don't always get exactly the precise amount of B-complex needed in every mouse meal.

An important thing to watch is to make sure to adjust the water to the amount appropriate for the weight of meat you're using — you don't want the final product too dry or too soupy. Unless your cat likes it too dry or too soupy.

Buy quality salmon oil.

Essential Fatty Acids (EFAs) are extraordinarily important to overall health for cats. Cats in the wild get it from eating the brains and eyes of their prey. You're probably not feeding brains and eyes, and that's why you'll be using salmon oil. Don't let anyone try and tell you flaxseed oil is the "same." It's not. It works for dogs but not cats. Cats cannot process the EFAs from flaxseed oil into something that's bioavailable for them.

When and if you chunk the meat to include in your batches (versus grinding everything), go for chunks that are as big as your cat will eat—bigger is better. Try not to leave much or any skin on the chunks, as the fat is hard for kitty to tear through; if the cat gets a piece of fat stuck on her teeth she may become an "anti-chunk" cat altogether. My older cat Tubby eats around the fat in beef hearts, but my 1.5 month old kitten Kira eats them up with relish. I dont own a grinder so I use a cleaver to chop the meat into kitten-mouth sized pieces with my cleaver. Here's a tip for you based on my experience: if you are using a cleaver, it is easier to slice through semi-frozen bony meat than room temperature bony meat.

The more tearing at muscle meat they do, the better for their teeth and gums. Some cats are fussy and eat around the chunks at first. Leave them out for a little while. Many cats will go back and eat them a bit later. If that doesn't work, make the chunks smaller and slowly increase their size over time. Remember that cats eat mice and most cats I've don't go hunt down a grinder to process their mice into a pulp first. Mother Nature has cats eating mice and birds whole for a reason. It's not just the nutritional value, but for the overall health of the cat's mouth. Don't underestimate the value of the mechanical action of eating for these carnivores.

Chunking the muscle meat by hand goes faster if the meat is semi-frozen. If the time spent hand-chunking some of the meat is keeping you from enjoying life, buy a grinder and use that for grinding up the meat. You may want to use the smaller grinding plate for grinding bones if you're concerned that the size of bone bits is too big.

If you are doing something you find particularly distasteful, like cutting up a whole chicken, turn on some music and sing your heart out. Thank the animal you are chopping for nourishing your pet and adding years to her lifespan.

Storing and Serving Homemade Cat Food

Store the prepared food in something that is of a manageable size. Some folks store in freezer baggies. Others like those plastic freezer containers from Tupperware. A nice touch is to use wide-mouth Mason glass freezer jars. They keep the food fresh longer and it's always nice storing in glass instead of plastic. Be certain to buy the can-or-freeze jars, not the plain canning jars that are not freezer-safe.

I find the wide-mouthed, one-pint size of the can-or-freeze jars work perfectly for one- or two-cat households. I live with two cats, and I always have two containers in the refrigerator: the one we're using currently and another "on deck." When the first one is finished, I immediately take a new container out of the freezer and put it in the refrigerator to begin thawing. This works out well for two cats. How you opt to do this, of course, depends on how many cats you're feeding and how much they eat daily, which varies greatly from cat to cat. Another option some folks use is to freeze individual servings in ice cube trays, then remove and portion into individual baggies. If the food is a little frozen when you want to serve it, it's a snap to thaw it quickly in a baggie under hot water as you warm it. It's obviously better to have the food on the frozen side rather than the "starting to turn bad" side.

You might put a small label on each container with the food type (i.e., chicken, rabbit, whatever) and the date you made it. My rationale for doing this is that if I ever did end up with a batch that I suspect is bad, I know which containers contain the questionable batch.

Don't serve the food cold straight from the refrigerator. Some sensitive cats will hurl up their raw food if it's very cold when it hits their stomach. Buy some snack-size zipper baggies, portion the food into them, and run it under hot water until it's warmed to at least room temperature or slightly higher (i.e., mouse body temperature). Another method is to place the raw cat food bowl(metal/ceramic) into a bigger container with hot water.

I don't suggest microwaving this food. This is especially true if you've used bones in your recipe. Why would you want to cook something that's supposed to be served raw? Microwaving is the enemy of all the lovely nutrients and life-giving enzymes in raw food that you've just taken the time and trouble to prepare. Just warm the food under warm water or a place it in a hot bowl of water.

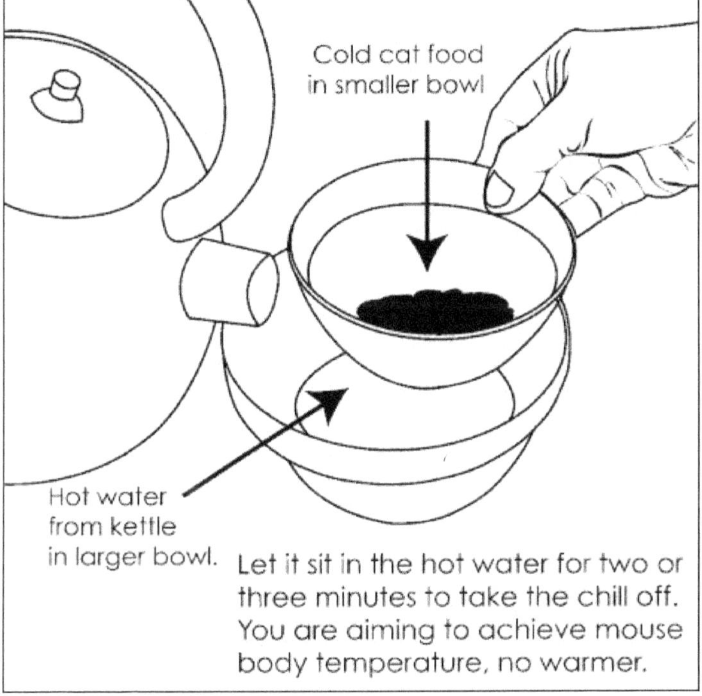

Important!

Never risk feeding food that is slightly "off" or spoiled. Chances are your cat won't touch it in that condition, but to be safe, you can try my trick: work out a thawing routine whereby the food you're about to serve is still just ever-so-slightly frozen. It's easy enough to complete the thawing quickly by running the food in a baggie under warm water to take off the chill, and this way you're assured that the food has not gone "bad" from being thawed for too long.

Fussbudget Felines

If your cat turns up her nose at the stuff, try not to fret too much. Do not give up. Just start by sneaking tiny amounts into canned or raw food and increase the amount slowly. Some cats take to raw food instantly, never look back, and seem relieved that you've finally figured out how to properly feed them. If that happens to you, count your blessings and don't worry about making the arduous, slow transition. However, some cats, especially older ones, are especially serious, dedicated, and stubborn kibble-addicts. Don't give in!

Do whatever it takes to get the cat eating her great new food–sprinkle ground up kibble on top if you must, but persist. Also remember: an otherwise healthy cat will NOT die from missing a few meals. Hunger can work in your favor. Don't be afraid to be a little stubborn.

Don't over-do the use of "bribe foods" on top of raw to get your cat eating the raw food, however. Lots of tuna juice, for example, is a big no-no, as the flavor is so powerful that your cat may refuse anything that isn't tuna flavored later on. But a sprinkle of their favorite old commercial food is fine. Another trick is to crumble some Freeze Dried Chicken crumbs on top of the new food.

Remember the important thing is to eventually make the transition, not to make it overnight. I took three full weeks to transition my first cat to raw, and I know of other people who have taken months to get their carbohydrate-addicted felines fully switched to this diet. It's all much easier if we start feeding this way when they're young, adaptable kittens.

There is no need to change the diet if you're feeding a

kitten or an older cat, unless the older cat has CKD. There is no such thing as special “life stage” food for cats in the wild, like those you see on the shelves of many pet food superstores. A kitten will need definitely need more raw food, more finely chopped meaty bones and more frequent feedings, but not a different food. A senior cat that isn’t too active might need less food. But they all can thrive on good, healthy, fresh raw food.

A bit of variety is helpful in keeping house cats interested in their food. Good options include: rabbit, chicken, Cornish Game Hen, turkey, and guinea fowl. Some cats also love beef and lamb, but not all cats that have been eating commercial food for a long time digest beef or lamb easily at first.

Can *I* can actually make my own cat food?
Yes. You. Can.

“Isn’t making cat food time-consuming?“
Once you get a groove going and your supplies organized, not really. You’ll also likely spend a whole lot less time (and money) in veterinary clinics. If you can get a helper, go for it. Maybe hook up with a local friend and savor some special time together hacking up meat parts and grinding them while singing some tunes. Time spent making cat food is less than I used to spend fretting about my sick cat and trekking him to the vet when he’ll have a health issue. So yes, while it is definitely some work, it’s very manageable. Think of it as a labor of love.

◆◆◆

The initial assembly of the supplements and tools for making a home prepared raw diet for cats can seem a bit overwhelming. Bear in mind that once you've purchased many of the dry ingredients and supplements, they last a very long time. If you treat your grinder well, you should only have to buy it once. If you stock and organize supplies correctly at the start and keep them all in one place, you won't be running to the store or hunting down individual ingredients in multiple places every time you want to make a batch of food. Here's a link to all the cat supplements I buy. You can buy the same off Amazon or Tata 1mg App.

I feed a Prey Model Raw model, so I haven't invested in a meat grinder, but if you are planning on feeding Prey Model Raw Ground, you'll need the following:

Meat Grinder

A hard-working electric grinder is the single most important, time-saving tool you'll need if you're going to make cat food regularly and including ground bone. Being a bit of a control freak, I generally like grinding the meat and bones myself, thus sparing worry about whether someone else has kept his or her workspace and grinder parts spotlessly clean. Besides, if you want to grind meat WITH bone (which is really best), you'll probably need to buy a grinder yourself as most butchers won't grind bone for you.

You'll need the grinder for grinding the raw bone and some of the meat attached to it, but an important part of raw feeding includes leaving plenty of nice fat chunks of muscle meat in the food for kitty to chew. Please remember, it's best to "chunk" a good portion, if not all, of the muscle meat by hand, to give kitty a chance to do some serious chewing to help keep her teeth and gums in good health. If your cat is missing a large number of teeth, or if you are feeding a 1 month old kitten, however, you may want to grind everything.

Few grinders are guaranteed for use in grinding bone. Search for 'meat grinder' and 'kheema machine' on amazon. Please note that the manufacturer instructions say to NOT attempt to grind bones. For what it's worth, the machines aren't guaranteed for grinding bones. You'll have to decide whether you want to fork over more money for a heavier-duty grinder that won't be out of warranty if you grind bones.

You could quite easily store your grinder and all the supplies and supplements used for cat food making in the same cupboard space that was once filled with cans and bags of commercial cat food.

Again, PLEASE be advised that grinding bones is NOT what most grinders are designed for. I've found that using my grinder for its "unintended purpose" works just fine — I've put pounds of meat and bone through my grinder for a year with absolutely no troubles. Please remember that you should always wash your grinder parts by hand, and not in a dishwasher.

You have some choices out there in the world of grinders. And, to my mind, it's really not necessary to spend a fortune for a grinder that will do a perfectly fine job for you. Yes it's an investment, or at least it can seem so at first. But it's still likely to be cheaper than multiple prescription medications and veterinary visits for all manner of nutrition-related ailments.

Meats and Organs

If you want meats that are free-range, antibiotic-free, and

hormone-free, a decent chain in the United States and Canada is Whole Foods Market. They also sell very nice organic chicken liver, so pick up fresh liver there as well. Sourcing hearts can be tricky, but it's well worth the effort. You will have to call around to see if you can find someone who will keep you supplied with hearts.

It's possible to get wonderfully fresh whole rabbit, delivered freshly-frozen direct to your door. I sometimes order rabbit from My Karnataka Ham Shop in Banglore. If you're on the US West coast, another great supplier that serves that area and that will deliver directly to your door is Wholefoods4pets. They're located in Washington state. In Bangalore, New Karnataka Ham Shop and Fresh2Home has rabbit, quail and turkey.

Try and search out free-range meats that are not administered "preventive" antibiotics or growth hormones. If you can't find "organic" meats, then at least try to use liver from a good source (i.e., no antibiotics or hormones and from a free-range animal) because the liver stores all the body's toxins and a non-free-range, overmedicated animal will be packed with toxins. Same goes for eggs -buy eggs from cage-free, unmedicated hens. *Naati* Eggs are perfect. Animals raised in humane conditions aren't right on top of one another's feces. They live in naturally cleaner conditions with access to the natural disinfectant action of the sun and are much less prone to the diseases that mass-production farms are continually vaccinating against and administering antibiotics for. Your cat has no use for second hand antibiotics, vaccinations or growth hormones. Your cat is a carnivore and needs quality untainted meat deemed fit for human consumption, at the least.

My cat food "repertoire" of flavors includes: whole chicken, whole rabbit, whole quail, lean beef, and batches made with just chicken thighs (with bone, of course). When the cats in my house were treated to their first meals of quail, I got a eight paws up on that.

The sometimes vexing chicken heart issue.

You'll note that the recipe that I use calls for chicken hearts. I am a big believer in trying to use real organ meats to supply some of the key nutrients needed in a healthy carnivore diet. No one will ever convince me you can duplicate Mother Nature's genius using isolated supplements. It's possible to improvise and use store-bought supplements to make up for that if you cannot source organs, but hunting down the real thing is worth a bit of your time.

Lots of people – at first- have faced a hard time sourcing organs. Please don't give up too soon if you can't immediately source real heart–it is such a magnificent source of real taurine and so many other rich, health-giving nutrients that are wonderful for our carnivore friends. That said, please don't not try this diet just because you can't find chicken hearts. Go ahead and follow the instructions for adding additional taurine if you come up dry in your hunt for hearts.

Fresh To Home in Bangalore carries chicken hearts. Best of all, the hearts came in oh-so-convenient 500gm packages, which can be bagged into smaller portions when you receive them(Fresh To Home sells their meat refrigerated, but not frozen).

Vitamins and Such

Psyllium

This is easy. Almost any regular grocery store or health food store carries containers of plain whole psyllium husks or psyllium husk powder. It's available on Amazon too. Remember to get loose powder rather than capsules that you need to individually open. You can also order psyllium husks from plenty of places online.

You'll note on the recipe that I use that not all cats require or benefit from adding psyllium into their diet. If your cat has been eating low-quality commercial food for several ears, especially dry food, she may have lost bowel elasticity and may benefit from the extra fiber. As a general rule, I recommend using psyllium when an adult cat first gets raw food, particularly if the cat has been eating a lot of dry food. At least one study suggests that cats on processed, cooked diets lose bowel elasticity over time, so it can be a good idea to try psyllium and then judge whether or not to continue based on your cat's stools.

I never add psyllium on all days to the food. Some cats seem to get constipated without additional fiber, whereas other cats seem to get constipated if they get too much fiber. Each cat is unique, and you'll have to judge which works best for your cat.

Salmon Oil

If you can procure wild salmon oil (versus farmed) that has high concentrations of EPA (Eicosapentaenoic Acid) and DHA (Docosahexaenoic Acid), then do that. I'm also fond of the Carlson brand of salmon oil, which has nice high levels of EPA and DHA and is free of detectable levels of mercury, cadmium, lead, PCBs and 28 other contaminants. Remember that salmon oil degrades quickly, so serving it fresh from a newly opened capsule is best. In addition to adding it to the recipe itself, I also squeeze some drops of salmon oil from capsules on to prepared food a few times a week. Most cats adore the flavor and it's nice to get the fresh oil into them regularly. Just clip the end of the capsule with a small scissors or pierce it with a sharp safety pin/dot pin and squeeze a few drops on to the food.

I strongly suggest that you steer clear of salmon oil that comes as a liquid in a bottle. That oil can go rancid very fast once it is exposed to air, even if it comes in one of those lovely cobalt-blue bottles that's supposed to protect the product. It's really best to buy capsules or very small bottles(for eg: kids' size Mercola Krill oil) instead.

Remember–your cat needs an animal-based source of Essential Fatty Acids. Don't let anyone tell you that flaxseed oil or another kind of plant-based EFA source works as well. It doesn't. Your cat is a carnivore and cannot derive all that she needs EFA-wise from plant based sources. There are many ways in which cats function differently biochemically from dogs. Cats, for example, cannot make their own Arachidonic Acid even when there is linoleic acid present. A cat's "chemical factory" (liver), contains no delta-6 desaturase enzyme to make the conversion of linoleic acid to Arachidonic acid. And there is little or no Arachidonic acid in plant matter. A dog, on the other hand, if consuming the proper fats, can make Arachidonic acid. Cats would normally get ample EFAs from eating the brains and eyes of her prey. So unless you're feeding brains and eyes, don't use flaxseed to get EFAs into your cat.

Glandular Supplement

Many folks have a hard time finding a good glandular supplement – don't sweat it if you are already feeding glands and can't find it. Just skip it. but what I use is Nutricology Immoplex. What I like about it is that it comes in capsules (versus tablets) which means it's simple to pull the capsules apart. This is much easier than crushing a tablet in a mortar and pestle. More importantly, I like this brand because unlike many other glandulars, it contains a good variety of raw tissue concentrates including spleen, brain, liver, heart, kidney, thymus, adrenal, pituitary, pancreas, and duodenum.

If the glandular supplement you purchase comes in tablets, you can crush them in a mortar and pestle or, if you don't have those tools, put them in a plastic baggie, wrap it in a towel, and smash them up with a hammer. See why I like the capsules? So much easier.

Remember, do not simply buy anything labeled a "glandular supplement." Many of these products are made from plants, herbs, or other food supplements. You're not looking for something with various herbs to help glandular health in humans; you ARE looking for a something that CONTAINS actual glands and nothing else. Read the ingredients at the back of the bottle.

Vitamin E and Vitamin B-50 Complex

These are very easy to source at any health food store or online.

Taurine

I use loose powdered taurine from NOW

Relax. You Can Make Cat Food.

I'm No Whiz in the Kitchen

Nor do I always cherish spending lots of time there. But making homemade cat food is something that's much easier than you might think. It's certainly much easier than I thought it would be when I started this adventure way back in the olden days of 2020. Trust me: Everything's going to be okay.

Look at it this way: the so-called professionals who put those fancy labels on their cans and bags with AAFCO nutritional guarantees are the same ones who let tainted wheat and heaven-knows-what else get into food and poisoned thousands of cats and dogs in early 2007. You know you can most likely do better than that.

It's a matter of being organized about your foodmaking supplies and then:

1. Getting out the grinder.
2. Assembling the ingredients from the recipe.
3. Chunking the muscle meat (i.e., cutting at least some of the meat into chunks that will not be ground), if you opt to do that.
4. Grinding the bones and other remaining meat on bones together with the organ meat (heart and liver), if you opt to feed PMR ground.
5. Adding the vitamins, egg yolks, and other ingredients in the recipe to the water and whisking that all up. My ingredient list is here.
6. Mixing it all together.
7. Spooning the mix into freezer-safe containers. I use a measuring cup to dole into wide-mouth jars.
8. Crowing righteously about how cool you are for making healthy cat food.
9. That's all. You're done.

It's that simple. Now go clean up your kitchen, serve up some food—warm it in a baggie under warm water—to your grateful cats, and go listen to some soothing music.

Total time? Obviously, that depends on how fast you are. I've been making cat food for over 2 years now and I have the process of making a batch that lasts two cats for about two weeks down to just about exactly one hour, including cleanup, taking out the trash, pausing for stretches, singing songs, etc. Truth be told, since my partner joined the cat foodmaking staff a few years ago, together we whip out a big ol' batch (triple or quadruple the recipe on this site) in 30 or 40 minutes together, particularly if we buy whole cut up chickens.

If you, like me, have a supplier you fully trust that will grind everything, including bone, the time involved is much shorter. The family that makes cat food together stays together and spends a lot less time and money in veterinary clinics. If you can get a helper, go for it. Maybe find a local friend and enjoy some special time together hacking up meat and grinding it and listening to show tunes.

Hot Tip!

My hot 'new' tip, which I can't believe took me well over a decade to figure out, is to not open individual capsules (so time consuming) but put them in a cup of warm water and let them dissolve. If you get impatient, you can use an immersion blender to emulsify quickly.

CHAPTER TEN

PREY MODEL RAW (PMR) FEEDING GUIDE

If you're reading this, you've probably already seen the research in the previous chapters and realize how important a species-appropriate diet is for your cat; I won't have to bore you with the kibble-is-bad lecture and can move right into giving you the scoop on what is good for your furry little friends.

Which is to say, a raw, prey-based or -modeled diet. Cats are obligate carnivores and, in the wild, live on rodents, birds, reptiles and insects. A prey-based diet seeks to mimic that menu by providing either whole prey animals or enough meats, organs, bones, etc. from different animal sources to recreate the same nutrient balance as would be found in a whole prey animal(franken-prey, if you will).

Raw diets can be procured in two ways – commercially or at home. This chapter discusses homemade prey model raw whole diet.

Part 1 - Methodologies

There are three primary methodologies for preparing a raw diet: ground PMR, whole PMR and Whole Prey. The first two are based on a general guideline that has been used by raw dog feeders for decades, modified for cats – the 83/

7/5/5 rule – that's 83% meat, fat, skin, sinew, connective tissue and heart, 7% edible bone, 5% liver, and 5% other secreting organ. The third – Whole Prey is as close to natural as your cat can get without catching dinner on its own. Rodents are roughly 5% bone and 4% liver, rabbits are slightly less than 10% bone and less than 4% liver. Birds have an even lower bone and organ content.

Grinding is the most well-known and popular method. It is the farthest from a "natural" diet in that the meats, organs, bones, etc. are all ground together, offering little to no chewing challenge to a cat and, due to the nutrient breakdown inherent in the process, requiring supplementation. However, this method most resembles the canned food many cats are already accustomed to eating and is often the easiest raw transition a cat can make. Cats are notoriously picky and some take weeks, months, or even years to recognize whole prey or prey model as food, or accept the work inherent in eating them. Sometimes, they're brought to raw at an older age and are missing teeth or too young when they should be nursing. In these cases, appropriately supplemented ground diets provide the incredible nutritional benefits of eating a species-appropriate diet (if not the dental and psychological benefits) and are a good interim step.

As grinding is the most prevalent raw feeding methodology, there are several detailed how-to articles and recipes already available online (see Feline-Nutrition.org, CatInfo.org and CatNutrition.org for the most well-known and vetted recipes).

Prey Raw model(PMR) Wholel (sometimes also called

Frankenprey) is not as widely known, but is slowly becoming more mainstream. In this method, a variety of animal parts are fed in measured amounts so that over a certain period of time (usually a week), the cat gets the same sum of parts as it would have were it eating whole animals. Meals are often all meat or a mix of meat with bone or organ and are fed in large chunks that the cat must actively gnaw on to reduce to bite-size pieces.

This active engagement in the eating process has several benefits to the cat, including the psychological satisfaction inherent in successfully meeting mental and physical challenges (eating becomes work!). One of its more important benefits, however, is improved dental health. Dental disease is at near-epidemic proportions in the feline population and has far-reaching health consequences for the cat. A diet that includes tearing, ripping and scissoring through meat, tendons and bones provides the necessary stimulation to keep your carnivore's mouth clean and healthy. (Unfortunately, a raw diet may not undo past damage or remove already built-up plaque or tartar, so your raw-fed cat may still need a cleaning at some point.) In addition, the very act of scissoring chunks off fresh raw protein sets off a chain reaction that releases a more efficient combination of enzymes in the cat's digestive system (starting with the enzymes in saliva!) and this, combined with the extended time required to finish a meal, promotes a better digestive process.

Feeding Whole entails less initial preparation than grinding, minimal or no supplementation because the nutrients are not lost in the process of grinding, and fewer tools, but it requires strict adherence to a feeding schedule to ensure the proper nutrient balance is maintained.(You can see a sample feeding menu at the end of this chapter)

Whole prey is the rarest raw feeding method. It is exactly what it sounds like – whole animals such as mice, rats, young chicks, and quail are offered to your cat. It is, obviously, the most natural method, but it is the least acceptable to both cat owners – who sometimes find it emotionally difficult to handle dead animals – and the cats themselves, who often have trouble recognizing the prey as food (accustomed as they are to heavily processed kibble and / or canned products). If both owner and cat can get past these difficulties, whole prey is the easiest, most efficient and most beneficial method of raw feeding.

Frozen chicks from an online store that sells retile food.Credits: Thelittlecarnivore.com

As in any topic, there are proponents of the various methods who eschew all others as being inferior. Don't let these well-meaning but sometimes overly-passionate folks intimidate or discourage you – all three feeding methods (and any combination there-of) are healthy, nutritious and far, far better for your cat than even the "best" commercially manufactured foods.

Menu Choices and Product Preparation

Whichever method you choose to use, a variety of animals should be part of the menu. This will keep the cats from losing interest in particular foods, but, more importantly, it maintains a better nutritional balance. Nutrient profiles differ between prey animals and what is low in one may be high in another. Chicken, for instance, is high in fat, while rabbit is very lean; quail is high in copper and chicken breast is high in niacin. Even different parts of the same animal can have different nutrients. Offering a variety of animals provides the greatest assurance of a balanced diet and mimics the hunting behavior of cats in the wild.

Turkey, chicken, Cornish hen, beef, lamb and pork are often basic ingredients and can be readily found in local stores. Many raw feeders don't feed pork because of parasite concerns but I've seen that cats do fine. Pork contains some nutrients not found in other meats. Venison, bison, pheasant, quail, rabbit, duck and goat can sometimes be found locally, but can also often be ordered online.(Fresh to home has Quail, Turkey. Protein Fresh has buffalo)

Liver, kidney and other organs can be sourced from any animal and do not need to "match" the meat products; it's fine to feed beef chunks, chicken liver and lamb heart in a single meal. Your goal is to recreate a whole animal from different animals.

Organic products are just as much healthier for your cat

as they are for you, but feeding organic is not a critical component of a raw-fed regimen. Organic or not, however, care must be taken that any product destined for your cat's plate is not "enhanced" with extra sodium or flavorful marinades. The sodium content should not exceed "80mg per serving" as written on the package. Human-grade marinated meats will not work

Prey model and whole prey feeding methodologies do not require a great deal of preparation.
Boneless products (beef, pork, heart, organs, etc.) need to be cut down to whatever size your cat is comfortable with, then weighed into meal-sized portions and packed in labeled freezer bags or freezer-safe plastic containers. Organs don't generally make up a whole meal, so add as much meat necessary to reach the desired portion size.

Pork, kidney, and sometimes heart have thick clumps of fat; it's not necessary to remove every single bit of this fat, but removing most of it is generally a good idea for weight maintenance and to ensure the cat is getting the intended amount of protein as too much fat can interfere with protein absorption.(Unless you have a kitten, in which case let the fat be.) If you get premixes labelled 'Pet Feast', give it in small amount as most butcher-shop made 'pet feasts' are very high in fat.

Bone-in meats with small edible bones – Cornish hen, quail and chicken ribs, wings, necks and backs, for instance – can be cut into single cat portions using kitchen shears and then packed for the freezer. Meats with weight-bearing bones such as turkey drumsticks and chicken leg quarters can either be packed for the freezer as they are and the meat cut off the bones at serving time, or de-boned, weighed and packed for the freezer in single cat portions, depending on your needs.

Because weight-bearing bones are difficult for cats to break, many cat owners do not feed them. However, whacking a large bone with a hammer is a perfectly acceptable way to reduce it to more manageable pieces. Always feed bones with meat on them, as this will encourage the cat's interest and, more importantly, make it easier and safer for the cat to digest. Never feed bones that are meant for larger animals like dogs to cats.

<u>Never feed cooked bone, as it can splinter and cause serious complications.</u>

Whole prey products are often purchased already frozen, so your prep work will likely be limited to separating the animals into meal-size portions and re-packing them for the freezer. In the wild, felines don't normally eat the stomach contents of their prey unless they're starving, and since our domesticated cats don't often find themselves that hungry, you may need to gut the prey before offering it to your cat. In addition, some cats find the urge to play with prey animals irresistible – in these cases, using kitchen shears to reduce the prey-animal into smaller pieces may make such play less tempting.

Due to a variety of factors, including toxins, thaimine-depleting antinutrients and histamines, fish shouldn't make up more than a very small percentage of your cat's diet. Feed only wild-caught varieties, not farm-raised, to avoid antibiotics, and make sure they are packed in water with no added salt. Sardines, invariably wild-caught (often in a sustainable manner), are among the safest to feed. They grow to adult size quickly, live only six or seven years, and eat mostly plants, all of which limits their exposure to PCBs, mercury and other heavy metals and toxins. They are full of Omega 3 fatty acids, making them a valuable – if minimal – contribution to your cat's diet (once a week is great!). Insects can be a fun addition to a cat's menu, too. Just throw a few crickets in the bath tub once or twice a month and watch your kitty go into hunting mode.

One issue that crops up with prey model and whole prey diets that is seldom, if ever, seen with ground is the runaway dinner. The larger the piece of food you offer and the more it resembles whole prey, the more likely it seems the cat is to run off with it. The most effective method to reduce or eliminate this behavior is to separate cats by levels and distance. Buy a small table and feed one cat on the table and one on the floor and/or feed cats on opposite sides of the room; this helps the cats relax and allows them to feel less threatened. If necessary, and your cats tolerate the confinement, you can crate them separately for meals.

Always defrost your cat's food in the fridge, not on the counter. Bacteria grow faster at room temperatures than they do in the fridge and while your cat is far less likely to become ill from this than you are, it's good practice not to do it since most cats will turn their noses up to even slightly off meat. Whether you serve food straight from the fridge or slightly warmed depends on your cat's preferences. If necessary, you can take the chill off your cat's dinner by sealing it in a bag and placing it in warm water for a few minutes. Don't put the food directly into the water, as this leaches nutrients out, and make sure the water is only warm, not hot, as hot water will cook the outside of the meat and degrade the nutrient content. Microwaving is not recommended for the same reason – the instant you turn it on, it begins cooking the food and destroying nutrients.

With the single exception of Omega-3 fats, supplements are not generally necessary in prey model and whole prey diets. Beef and poultry used to be raised on grasses and other greens, leading to higher levels of Omega-3s in their tissues, however, today's animals are often corn and soy fed, creating a higher Omega-6, lower Omega-3 balance. If not compensated for, this can lead to an imbalance in a raw-fed cat's diet.

Feeding grass-fed meat sources whenever you can will help prevent this, as will offering Sardines once a week. The heads of prey animals are also good to feed, as brains and eyes are both high in Omega-3s.

Alternatively, you can purchase wild-caught Salmon Oil or Small Fish Oil and drizzle 1000mg or so over the cat's food two or three times a week. Buy capsules rather than liquid products, as the oil tends to break down fairly quickly once the container is opened. Stay away from cod liver oil – it can be high in Vitamin A and in conjunction with the liver already being offered, could push those levels too high – and avoid non-animal-sourced oils such as flax and grape seed.

Some Things To Know As You're Creating Your Cat's Weekly Menu:

– The harder a muscle works, the higher its taurine content. For example, chicken thighs have more taurine than chicken breasts, and heart, of course, has the highest taurine content. Feeding heart a couple of times a week is

a great way to ensure your cat is getting all the taurine it needs. And taurine is water soluble, so there's no worry about over-feeding it.
– Skin is quite fatty, so watch your cat's weight and cut back if necessary. Chicken skin is especially high in fat. Chicken fat is high in PUFA's.
– Gizzards are tough to chew, which makes them great for exercising your cat's jaws or slowing down a fast eater.
– Rabbit is generally a very lean protein source. Cats require more fat in their diet than we do (20% – 35%), so, while rabbit is great as a part of the diet, it shouldn't be the sole protein source.
– Beef, pork, lamb, bison, and venison are completely acceptable meat ingredients, but some cats may be reluctant to eat them. Most raw feeders happily feed these products, but a few balk at doing so, saying such prey is "unnatural". Contradicting this, however, are historical accounts describing the African black-footed cat killing and eating sheep and goats. This cat is a genetic ancestor to our own, so these accounts should put to rest any doubts about feeding products from hoofed animals.1
– Whole eggs are fine as occasional additions, but be aware that too much at one time may cause loose stools.

Part 2: Putting It Into Action
How Much to Feed

To determine how many ounces of raw food to feed, multiply your cat's weight in Pounds by 16 to convert it to ounces and then multiply that by 2%, 3% or 4%. Divide that total by however many meals you offer each day to get the ounces to feed per meal (until they are about a year old, kittens can generally be offered twice this amount). Feeding three times a day (four for kittens) is a better option than feeding twice a day, as the cat's stomach may become too acidic if it goes hungry for too long, causing digestive upsets and possible vomiting.

Your starting percentage depends on your cat's current weight and activity level; the leaner the cat and the higher the activity level, the higher the percentage you start with. If you're not sure what percentage is best, start with 3% and adjust as needed. You should be able to feel your cat's ribs, but not actually see them. If you can't feel them, slowly reduce how much you feed; if you can see them, slowly increase how much you feed.

For example, an overweight, inactive 15.5 pound cat would be fed about 4.96 ounces of food a day (15.5 x 16 = 248; 248 x 2% = 4.96) , while a lean, active 10 pound cat would be offered about 6.4 ounces (10 x 16 = 160; 160 x 4% = 6.4).

Once you know how much raw to offer your cat each day, your next step is to determine how much of what part to feed. You can do this using daily numbers, but it's easier to calculate by the week, so take that daily total from above and multiply it by 7 to get a weekly total. (Continuing the previous example of the overweight cat: 4.96 x 7 = 34.72 ounces of food per week.)

Now multiply that weekly total by:
83% = ounces of meat to feed each week
7% = ounces of bone to feed each week
5% = ounces of liver to feed each week
5% = ounces of non-liver organ to feed each week

Still using the 15.5 pound kitty example, as well as the more generally recommended %'s (as shown here), we get the following:

83% = 27.78 ounces of meat to feed each week (34.72 x .83 = 28.82)

7% = 3.47 ounces of bone to feed each week (34.72 x .07 = 2.43)

5% = 1.74 ounces of liver to feed each week (34.72 x .05 = 1.74)

5% = 1.74 ounces of non-liver organ to feed each week (34.72 x .05 = 1.74)

This is the part that often discourages new raw feeders before they've even begun, but these calculations need only be done once. Once the diet is established, you can easily tweak the numbers if and as needed. If you want to do what I do: feed by percentages, keep an eye out for my next book which will explore this.

Note that for raw-feeding purposes, meat, fat, skin, sinew, connective tissue, hearts, lung and gizzards are all considered muscle meat. They count toward the muscle meat percentage, not the organ requirement.

Liver has its own requirement and the remaining non-liver organ percentage can consist of kidney, spleen, testicles, brain, eyes, pancreas – any secreting organ in the body. As mentioned earlier, the more variety you offer, the better the nutritional profile you are offering your cat.

Determining how to fit the appropriate amount of bone into your cat's diet can take a bit of work, but a review of the USDA's chart (5) will give you the bone-to-meat ratio of many of the most commonly fed raw products and can be used to calculate your needs. Chicken wings, for instance, are 46% bone and 52% everything else. A tubby kitty needs

3.47 ounces of bone per week, so he would need to eat a total of 7.5 ounces of chicken wings every week (3.47 / .46 = 7.54 rounded up to 7.5oz), which breaks down to 2.5 ounces of chicken wings three times a week (7.5oz / 3meals = 2.5oz per meal).

Among other things, bone is necessary to keep a cat's digestive system regulated, so you want to feed it fairly often; a minimum of three feedings a week is good. If you feed it less often, you may end up with a cat whose stools that are alternately too hard – which can cause discomfort or even constipation – or too soft – which can be uncomfortable for both of you. If you're feeding the 7% weekly requirement in three feedings and your cat's stool still seems to be too hard, you can cut back to the lower end of the recommendation (down to 5%). Don't panic if your cat's stools drop in frequency, however, as a drop in waste quantity is to be expected on a raw diet. Many raw fed cats can go a day or two between stool deposits and some even longer. My raw fed kitten pees more than she poops, and her poops are tiny! There is zero poop smell in my room when she goes in her litter box. The only smell I get while cleaning the litter tray is ammonia.

The liver percentage is generally given as 5%, but that, too can be lowered, down to 3%. It's a good idea not to exceed the 5%, though, because liver is a great source of Vitamin A, which can be toxic if overfed. This is why some kitties have loosies after eating liver. Though the level required to reach toxicity varies by cat, it is generally such a high amount that it's an unlikely event, but it's best to exercise caution by not overfeeding liver.

Also, some cats find liver and other organs a bit "rich" and may get diarrhea if they eat too much at a single sitting, so, like bone, it's a good idea to spread these out over two or more meals per week.

Sample Cat Meals

I know what I wanted most when I first started was examples, so here are three. The prey model raw is what my cats are currently eating and the prey model ground is basically what they started out eating. As you read these examples, keep in mind the meals are split between six cats.

Prey Model Raw

Breakfast:

– Monday, Wednesday and Friday = 10oz of chicken, duck and turkey heart, respectively.

– Tuesday and Saturday = 10oz of beef round or stew chunks.

– Thursday and Sunday = 10oz of pork loin chunks.

Lunch:

– Monday, Wednesday, and Saturday = bone-in meals: 6 chicken wings (minus the drummettes), ~15oz of chicken ribs w/meat still attached and another ~15oz of small rabbit bones w/meat still attached, respectively.

– Tuesday and Friday = 6oz of liver and 6oz of gizzards.

– Thursday and Sunday = 6oz of kidney and 6oz of chicken breast meat.

Dinner:

– Monday and Thursday = 10oz of rabbit meat.

– Tuesday and Saturday = a turkey drumstick

– Wednesday and Sunday = a chicken leg quarter.

– Friday = 9 boned and mostly skinned chicken wing drummettes.

Every Friday they share a single 3.75oz can of sardines, on Saturday they get either egg yolks or egg whites and on Sunday they share a couple dozen live crickets.

Prey Model Raw- Ground
Breakfast:
– A ground mix of the weekly requirements of bone, liver and organ, with the appropriate supplements and enough additional meat to equal a total of 70oz, divided into seven, 10oz meals and fed each morning.
Lunch:
– About 10oz of gizzards, chicken or beef heart, beef round, or pork loin.
Dinner:
– About 10oz of chicken breast, or a turkey drumstick or chicken leg quarter.
Weekend treats could be the same as on prey model.

Whole Prey, Prey Model & Ground
Breakfast:
– A ground mix of the weekly requirements of bone, liver and organ, with the appropriate supplements and enough additional meat to equal a total of 70oz, divided into seven, 10oz meals and fed each morning.
Lunch:
– Six adult mice, small rats, baby chicks, small quail, etc.
Dinner:
– About 10oz of any of the prey model products from the first two examples.
Weekend treats could be the same, again.

Equipment and Cleaning
To feed prey model and whole prey, you'll need a scale that

registers down to a quarter of an ounce or less, a good set of kitchen shears, a high-quality medium or large carving knife, a knife sharpener (skin dulls a knife fast!!), cutting board and freezer bags and / or freezer storage containers. You'll also find that freezer space is a huge convenience; you can shop, chop, bag and freeze once a month with a freezer large enough.

You can scrub down your preparation area with disinfecting wipes, then thoroughly rinse and dry it with paper towels, which is easier and more thorough than cleaning with sponges or wash-clothes. Alternatively, you can use peroxide or a mix of vinegar and water to do the same thing. Always rinse thoroughly to prevent cats from picking up any of the disinfecting agents on their feet. If resources permit, using "green" products such as those made by Seventh Generation are a healthier and more ethical option.

Sourcing Products

– Ask about bulk purchasing everywhere you go. Watch for sales and marked-down meats.

– Check your local grocery stores first, you might be surprised at what they carry. Talk to the meat department; if they don't regularly stock what you want, they may be willing to bring it in once a month or so.

– Join a Costco, BJ's, Sams Club or other similar club store. Barter groups and coops usually have an annual cost, but everything you get is fresh – a benefit to your pets and your family.

– Ethnic Markets are often good sources for hard-to-find organs and meats.

– Tell your friends and relatives to ask around for hunters and fishers; let them know you're interested in animal parts they don't want.

– Talk to restaurants and caterers and ask for organs and other meat pieces they throw out. Also try restaurant suppliers.

– Call your local butcher and ask for the meats and organs they would normally throw out, including items that are nearing expiration.

– Online vendors are often pricey, but they can usually provide both pre-ground and whole prey products. If you purchase pre-ground products, make sure you know what, if any, supplements they add.

For the non-squeamish only...

– Local animal breeders and farmers. You may have to do so some of the cutting-up yourself, so be prepared.

– Slaughterhouses, meat and poultry packers and distributors. Ask for organ meats that normally get tossed. Also ask what else they throw away.

– Livestock auctions (the animals can be butchered for you).

Where NOT to get your foods...

– Craigslist and other ad venues are often suggested as good places to seek out hunting and fishing remains, old and/or freezer-burnt meats, etc., however, there are many unknowns in procuring products this way and, while you may save substantially on money, you are likely offering foods with a lower nutritional profile than you think. Many nutrients degrade over time in the freezer and some are even affected by light and / or air. Defrosting and refreezing exacerbates this process, so feeding products obtained this way can be risky.

– Road-kill not a good idea either, as the prior health state and current level of spoilage of the dead animals are unknown.

In Conclusion

There is a steep learning curve to home-preparing your cat's raw-food menu, but you'll be surprised after just a short time how easy it becomes. Your pet-related food and litter costs will drop and some otherwise-costly visits to the vet will almost assuredly be avoided. Your cats will be healthier, happier, and will live longer – a wonderful return on investment and well worth the effort involved.

CHAPTER ELEVEN

TROUBLESHOOTING THE TRANSITION

Many cat owners, already deeply sensitized to the potential risks of raw-feeding, panic when they run into a problem during the transition period. This is unfortunate, as the large majority of these problems are easy to address and not a reason for alarm. The same issues can occur whether you start with canned or kibble and switch to ground, prey model or whole prey raw foods, and a little patience and some detective work are all that's usually needed to identify and address the root cause.

Preventive strategies are always a good idea, and starting your cat on a healthy probiotic – one with 10 or more live strains of bacteria – a week or two in advance of the transition will help strengthen her digestive system and reduce the likelihood of digestive upsets. Taking the transition slowly and introducing one product at a time will further lower those chances.

Despite our best efforts, however, problems may still pop up. Here are the most commonly experienced issues, their potential causes and the most likely solutions.

Problem: Won't even try the new food.
Solution: Many times, cats raised on a life-time of canned mush or crunchy, coated kibble bits don't recognize raw foods as foods. The smell, taste and texture are very different, and feline instincts are naturally wary of eating anything unfamiliar.

Thankfully, cats can be "re-programed". Take a small dollop or chunk of the raw food you want your cat to start eating and place it next to her regular food at every meal. This will accustom her to the scent and sight of the raw food and help her begin to associate it with meals. Persistence will be your key and patience your greatest ally, as it can take a few days to over a month before she is willing to accept the raw as food.

Problem: Likes it; then doesn't.
Solution: Feline instinct also encourages cats to eat a variety of their familiar foods, and if fed the same product day after day, they may lose their taste for it. This is sometimes referred to as "the monotony effect." To prevent this, rotate through as many different animal meats as you can source.
Regular rotation of a variety of meats will also provide a stronger nutritional profile. A meta-study completed in 2008 concluded that our cats' bigger cousins, like the lion and the leopard, need between five and seven different prey types to meet their nutritional needs; although it is believed by most that a minimum of three or four is sufficient for house-cats, the more variety, the better.

Problem: Throwing up.

NOTE: Throwing up is a cat's natural response to a huge range of issues, from the simple to the life-threatening. If your cat can't keep anything down, hasn't eaten in over 48 hours or seems lethargic and/or feverish, veterinarian attention is recommended.

Solution: Throwing up within an hour or so after eating is referred to as regurgitation. Even limiting ourselves to discussing regurgitation-related vomiting only, there are many potential causes; in no instance, however, should recurrent regurgitation be considered normal. There is always a reason and it should be addressed to prevent further complications for the cat.

Cats are instinctively inclined to prefer warm foods and will sometimes regurgitate meals that are too cold, so ensure any food you offer is close to room temperature by taking the packaged food out of the fridge fifteen or so minutes early, or placing it in a bowl of warm (not hot) water for a few minutes.

Eating too fast, eating too much, and swallowing pieces that are too large all cause regurgitation. They are also related to going too long between meals, as happens frequently with cats that are fed only twice a day. Going too long without food can also create a build-up of stomach acid that will make the cat uncomfortable and nauseous, and can cause vomiting of yellow bile and white foam before a meal as well as regurgitation of a recently-eaten meal.

According to the National Research Council, cats would naturally eat between twelve to twenty meals in a twenty-four hour period. Dropping them down to three or four meals a day is a drastic reduction, but is tolerated more easily than only two. Feeding the first meal within a half-hour of rising (but NOT immediately after you get up, unless you want your cats to start waking you to be fed), right after you get home in the evening and again just before you go to bed works very well for most cats.

If your cat is still prone to hunger vomiting, giving her something small to nibble on while you're preparing her food will absorb some of the acid and make her more comfortable and less likely to get sick. Freeze-dried meat treats work really well for this.

Competition can also cause cats to eat too fast or swallow unacceptably large bites. Giving each cat her own plate, placing them further apart or feeding them on different levels, and ensuring they eat in uninterrupted quiet should alleviate their anxiety and help them slow down. Crating is also very helpful. With some cats, however, it may be necessary to feed them in separate rooms.

Cats new to prey model or whole prey foods are inexperienced and may bite off a larger piece than they can properly digest. The cat may make strange noises trying to swallow the food, and it will often come right back up to be re-chewed and swallowed again. Until the cat gains the necessary experience, cut her food down a bit before offering it to her.

In all of the above cases, it's perfectly acceptable to let the cat re-eat the food. If she doesn't do it on her own, you can sprinkle it with something enticing to encourage her. (This is easy to do when cats are crated for meals.)

If the cat is constipated or has a hairball problem, a full stomach will be uncomfortable and might result in regurgitation. Careful observance of litter box habits will help you recognize incipient constipation, and regular brushing will help prevent hairball issues. Neither of these issues occurs very often once a cat has been fully transitioned to a properly balanced raw diet.

If you're feeding a prey model raw diet and none of the above problems seem likely, check to ensure the meats and organs you've purchased are not enhanced. The sodium content should be no more than 100 mg per serving.

Problem: Constipation / Diarrhea.

Solution: Constipation is generally caused by too much bone in the diet. If you are feeding a commercial blend, call the manufacture for the product's bone to meat ratio; anything over 7% is high and should be diluted by adding fresh meat. If you are feeding a prey model raw diet using the 80/10/5/5 guideline, reduce the amount of bone in your bone-in meals from 10% to 7% (adult cats don't require the same amount of bone as do their canine counterparts. However, kittens need more bone than adult cats. If necessary, you can drop that even further to 5% for adult cats.

Diarrhea is encountered more often than constipation during raw-feeding transitions and can be a little more difficult to address. The spices in enhanced meats can cause loose stools, as can quality control issues in commercial ground mixes; the former you have control over, the later you don't. If you suspect an issue with a commercial raw food, switch to something else for a while.

Prey model raw feeders may be feeding too much fat, too many organ meats or too little bone – or some combination thereof. Double-check your numbers to ensure you're within the 83/7/5/5 guidelines, then tweak your cat's diet by adding a bit more bone, removing skin and other fat sources, or cutting back on organ meats.

Taking the transition too fast can also cause diarrhea. Add new products one at a time, even mixing them with current products if your cat seems to be particularly sensitive to changes in her diet. Be especially careful with organ meats; feed them in pea-sized amounts to begin with until you know your cat can handle them, and never feed a full meal only of organs.

Cats that have a history of digestive issues such as IBS and IBD need significantly slower transitions to allow their irritated and inflamed digestive systems plenty of time to adjust to eating their natural diet.

Conclusion

Providing your beloved kitty with the foods she is naturally designed to eat is probably the single most important choice you will ever make for her, but it isn't always a smooth transition. Preparing in advance, taking it slow, and being both patient and persistent will help ensure the best transition possible, and will pay off huge dividends in the long-term health of your cat.

Life stages, Lifestyles, and Cat Food

The number and types of commercial cat food seems multiplying. One online store carries 353 different dry foods, and 735 varieties of canned food! Here's a sampling of the lifestages cat food is made for:

- Babycat (0 to 4 months)
- Kitten (0 or 4 to 12 months)
- Adult (1 to 7 years)
- Mature (7 to 10 years)

- Senior (over 10 years)
- Young adult (from time of spay/neuter to 7 years)
- Young male (from time of neuter to 7 years)

In contrast, the American Association of Feline Practitioners (AAFP) has come up with its own lifestage classifications:

- Kitten (birth to 6 months)
- Junior (7 months to 2 years)
- Prime (3 to 6 years)
- Mature (7 to 10 years)
- Senior (11 to 14 years)
- Geriatric (15 years+)

This system divides lifestages by nutritional needs, behavior, and diseases common to each age group. It makes more sense in a way, because cats do tend to become overweight in middle age, and lose weight as seniors. But even AAFP recognizes that "any age groupings are inevitably arbitrary demarcations along a spectrum, and not absolutes." Then there are what I call "lifestyle" foods, including breed-specific diets. There are dozens of choices, including active, indoor, weight management, hairball, sensitive stomach, grain free, gluten free, urinary, kidney, hypoallergenic, multiple-cat, skin and coat, Siamese, Persian, Maine coon, and many more.

In addition, there are multiple food forms: dry, semi-moist, canned (including pouches), raw, dehydrated, freeze-dried, and homemade.

Pet food manufacturers also like to make quality claims to distinguish one from another. Today we have premium, super-premium, ultra-premium, gold, platinum, four-star, plus, extra, professional, prescription, human-grade, and of course, natural and organic. Except for the last two, there are no rules or definitions for any of these terms.

Yet after all is said and done, there are only TWO nutritional standards for cat food: adult and growth (kitten, pregnancy, lactation). "All life stages" foods comply with growth requirements. Everything else–everything–is purely marketing. The differences between these foods are primarily cosmetic–minor alterations in protein, fiber, and fat percentages, and perhaps one or more "glamour ingredients" such as blueberries, Omega-3 fatty acids, or kelp. These labels are designed to appeal to you, and have little to do with your cat's health. (For more info, check out articles on pet food labels and marketing hype.)

Now, think about the cat species for a moment, and consider how nature divides up the feline's lifestages. Young kittens and cubs, of course, nurse from their mom; this milk diet continues for 3 or 4 months, but after just a few weeks they are gradually introduced to solid food in the form of a variety of prey animals. And that's what they eat until their dying day. So the "natural" cat only has 2 nutritionally distinct stages: nursing, and the rest of their lives.

It's worth pointing out that, in nature, neither mother's milk nor prey animals are cooked, pasteurized, irradiated, kibbled, freeze-dried, or otherwise processed. Cat milk contains the sugar lactose albeit in smaller amounts than in cow's milk, which provides plenty of calories to support rapid growth; but once weaned, cats have no physiological need for carbohydrates. Their natural diet is grain-free, gluten-free, fresh, and raw; and it's good for their skin, coat, liver, teeth, body weight, activity, allergies, kidneys, bladder, and every other age, body part and condition.

So when you're choosing a cat food, don't fall for the hype. Get the best quality wet foods you can afford and that your cat will eat. Don't feed just one food all the time; cats need variety. Avoid foods containing "meat chunks" or "nuggets," "shreds," or other shapes, which are not meat at all but formed from texturized vegetable protein. Make sure your cat's food covers all life stages; this is the most appropriate standard. If you're still feeding dry or semi-moist food, today is a good day to start the transition to a better diet.

CHAPTER TWELVE

Sample Weekly Feeding Schedule for Adult Cats

Weekly Feeding Schedule

Day	Meal	Food
Monday	am	chicken hearts
	pm	chicken wings
	final	rabbit
Tuesday	am	beef
	pm	gizzards & liver
	final	chicken quarter
Wednesday	am	duck hearts
	pm	chicken/rabbit ribs
	final	turkey leg
Thursday	am	pork
	pm	chicken breast & kidney
	final	rabbit
Friday	am	turkey hearts
	pm	gizzards & liver
	final	chicken wing drummettes
Saturday	am	beef
	pm	chicken wings
	final	chicken quarter
Sunday	am	pork
	pm	chicken breast & kidney
	final	turkey leg

Wkly in ozs		Mthly (4 weeks) in lbs	
30	heart (10oz thrice)	7.50	heart
12	liver (6oz twice)	3.00	liver
12	gizzards (6oz twice)	3.00	gizzards
12	kidney (6oz twice)	3.00	kidney
12	breasts (6oz twice)	3.00	breasts w/ribs
20	beef (10oz twice)	5.00	beef
20	pork (10oz twice)	5.00	pork
20	rabbit (10oz twice)	5.00	rabbit
10	chicken wing pcs (10oz once)	2.50	chicken wing pcs
24	wings (12oz twice)	6.00	wings
15	chicken/rabbit ribs (15oz once)	3.75	breasts w/ribs
16	turkey drumsticks (8oz twice)	4.00	turkey drumsticks
16	chicken leg quarters (8oz twice)	4.00	chicken leg quarters
219		54.75	

Fri	one sardine each
Sat	two dozen crickets, shared
Sun	egg whites / yolks, alternated

Sample Weekly Feeding Schedule

Weekly Feeding Schedule for Adult Cats - With Price estimate

CatCentric

Better lives through better care!

Whole Prey Menu Example (with pricing estimate)

Weekly Feeding Schedule

Monday	am	quail
	pm	mouse
	final	rabbit
Tuesday	am	chick
	pm	mouse
	final	rat
Wednesday	am	quail
	pm	rat
	final	rabbit
Thursday	am	chick
	pm	mouse
	final	rat
Friday	am	quail
	pm	mouse
	final	rabbit
Saturday	am	chick
	pm	mouse
	final	rat
Sunday	am	chick
	pm	mouse
	final	rat

Weekly #'s	6		Monthly #'s	Cost @	Total Cost
36	6	jumbo or XL adult mice	144	$ 0.80	$ 115.20
30	5	small rat	120	$ 1.50	$ 180.00
24	4	day old chicks	96	$ 0.25	$ 24.00
18	3	pinkie rabbit	72	$ 1.00	$ 70.00
18	3	2 week quail	72	$ 1.00	$ 72.00
126			504		$ 461.20

Average cost per day per cat $ 2.56
(does not include shpg)

Fri one sardine each
Sat two dozen crickets shared
Sun egg whites / yolks alternated

*NOTE: This is for six cats. You can adjust as needed.

www.CatCentric.org

Enter Caption

Raw Feeding Pyramid

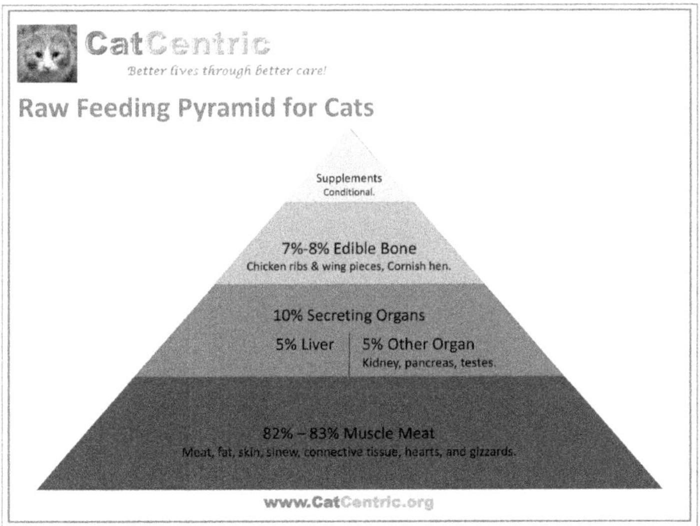

Enter Caption

Switching Your Cat to Raw Food - Step by Step

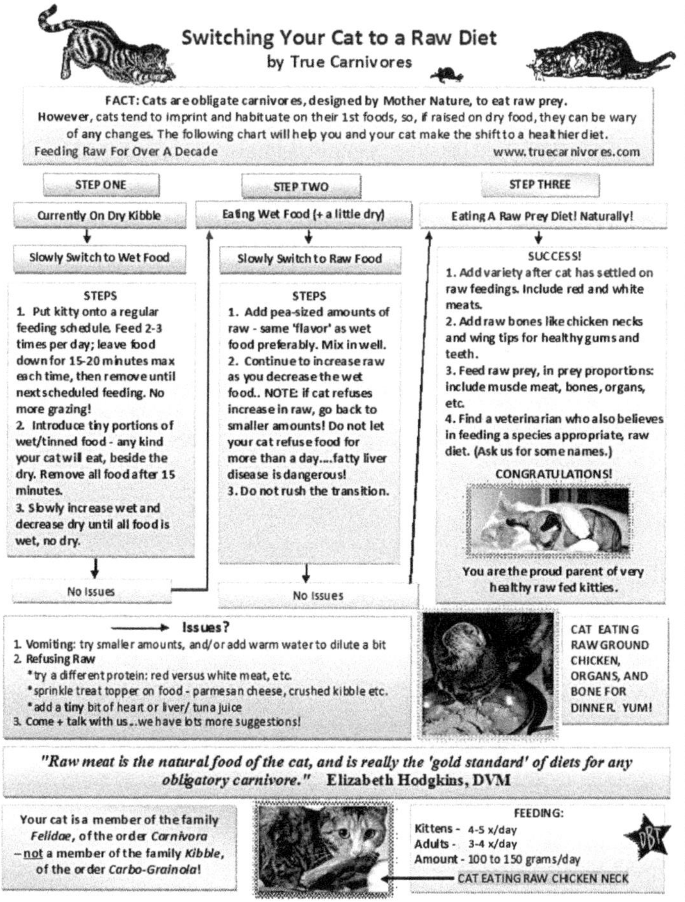

Enter Caption

PMR Cheat Sheet

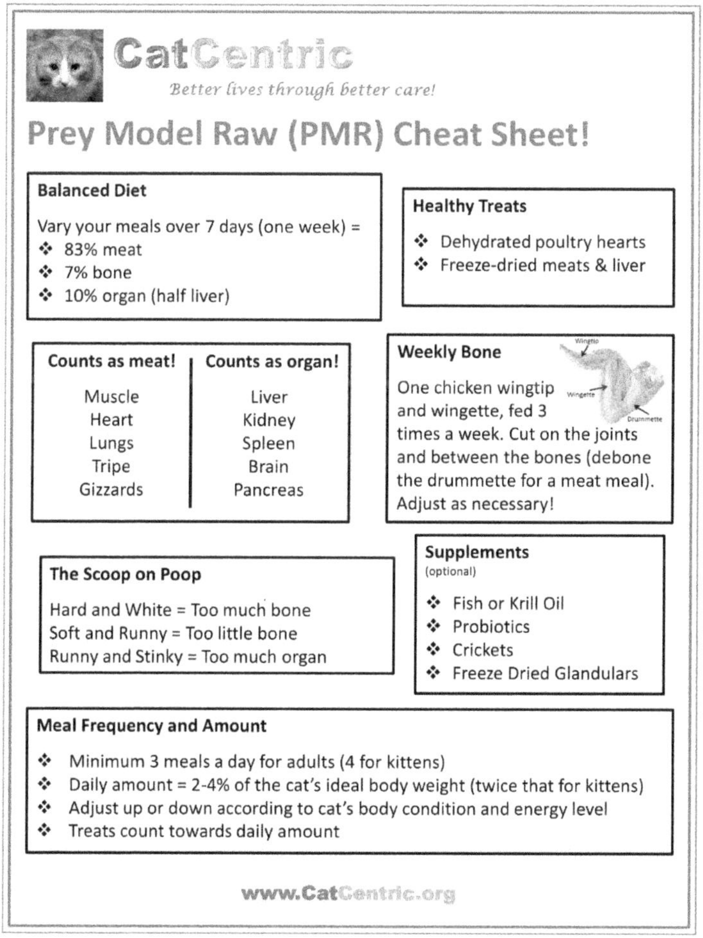

CatCentric

Better lives through better care!

Prey Model Raw (PMR) Cheat Sheet!

Balanced Diet

Vary your meals over 7 days (one week) =

- 83% meat
- 7% bone
- 10% organ (half liver)

Healthy Treats

- Dehydrated poultry hearts
- Freeze-dried meats & liver

Counts as meat!	Counts as organ!
Muscle	Liver
Heart	Kidney
Lungs	Spleen
Tripe	Brain
Gizzards	Pancreas

Weekly Bone

One chicken wingtip and wingette, fed 3 times a week. Cut on the joints and between the bones (debone the drummette for a meat meal). Adjust as necessary!

The Scoop on Poop

Hard and White = Too much bone
Soft and Runny = Too little bone
Runny and Stinky = Too much organ

Supplements
(optional)

- Fish or Krill Oil
- Probiotics
- Crickets
- Freeze Dried Glandulars

Meal Frequency and Amount

- Minimum 3 meals a day for adults (4 for kittens)
- Daily amount = 2-4% of the cat's ideal body weight (twice that for kittens)
- Adjust up or down according to cat's body condition and energy level
- Treats count towards daily amount

www.CatCentric.org

Enter Caption

Whole PMR Bone Guide

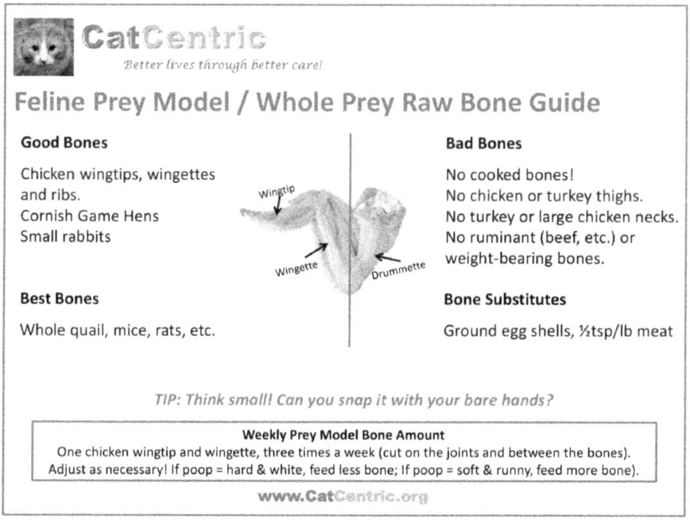
CatCentric

Better lives through better care!

Feline Prey Model / Whole Prey Raw Bone Guide

Good Bones

Chicken wingtips, wingettes and ribs.
Cornish Game Hens
Small rabbits

Best Bones

Whole quail, mice, rats, etc.

Bad Bones

No cooked bones!
No chicken or turkey thighs.
No turkey or large chicken necks.
No ruminant (beef, etc.) or weight-bearing bones.

Bone Substitutes

Ground egg shells, ½tsp/lb meat

TIP: Think small! Can you snap it with your bare hands?

Weekly Prey Model Bone Amount
One chicken wingtip and wingette, three times a week (cut on the joints and between the bones).
Adjust as necessary! If poop = hard & white, feed less bone; If poop = soft & runny, feed more bone).

www.CatCentric.org

Enter Caption

CHAPTER THIRTEEN

The British Pet Holocaust(1939-1945) & Emergency Cat Food Provisions.

The little-told story of the massive pet cull

- Just before WWII there were fears that war with Germany would result in food shortages.
- A British governmental committee recommended that pet dogs and cats be put to death to conserve food rations.
- Within the first four days of WWII, 400,000 pet dogs and cats were slaughtered.
- Later the government used relationships with pets as examples of British resilience, and erased the pet holocaust from memory.

The love that the British people have for their pets, especially dogs and cats, is so well-accepted that it is virtually recognized as part of the national character. Given that fact, how did the British needlessly slaughter 750,000 dogs and cats during World War II? Furthermore, how can it be that this event is so little-known and seldom discussed?

A True Holocaust

The full picture of what happened can be credited to Hilda Kean, a British historian who was the former Dean and Director of Public History at Ruskin College, Oxford.

Before we look at how it came about, it is important to understand the magnitude of what happened. In early September 1939, during the first four days of World War II, over 400,000 dogs and cats were killed. This number constituted some 26 percent of London's pets at the time. It is a number six times greater than the number of civilian deaths in the UK from bombing during the entire war. Furthermore by the time the campaign was finished this number would nearly double.

The Source of the Problem

We can trace this tragedy back to the summer of 1939. Britain declared war on Germany on September 3, 1939. However, the inevitability of the conflict was clear at the beginning of the year. For this reason, a number of defense committees were formed to prepare the nation should the British homeland become a target. One such was the National Air Raid Precautions Animals Committee (NARPAC).

NARPAC estimated that the pet population in England was around 6 to 7 million dogs and cats. The committee noted that the advent of war would mean, not only the potential for air raids but also the likelihood of food rationing and major food shortages. NARPAC worried that people would be tempted to share scarce food resources with their pets and thus declared that "to have a pet while the nation goes to war is an unaffordable luxury."

NARPAC published its recommendations in the pamphlet "Advice to Animal Owners." The pamphlet advised:

"If at all possible, send or take your household animals into the country in advance of an emergency." It concluded: "If you cannot place them in the care of neighbours, it really is kindest to have them destroyed."

As if to punctuate the seriousness of this suggestion, the inner cover of the pamphlet contained a full-page advertisement for the Cash Captive Bolt Pistol which was presented as "the standard instrument for the humane destruction of domestic animals."

The committee's advice was printed in almost every newspaper and announced on the BBC. During interviews with NARPAC committee members, some noted that they could even provide a rental service for such slaughter guns.

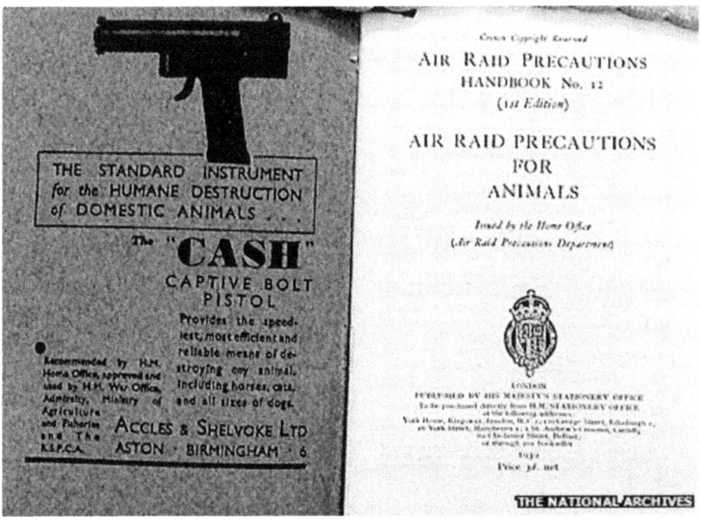

Source: National Archive/Wikimedia Commons Public Domain

The advice was printed in almost every newspaper and announced on the BBC. It was "a national tragedy in the making", says Clare Campbell, author of new book *Bonzo's War: Animals Under Fire* (1939 -1945). Campbell recalls a story about her uncle. "Shortly after the invasion of Poland, it was announced on the radio that there might be a shortage of food. My uncle announced that the family pet Paddy would have to be destroyed the next day."

After war was declared on 3 September 1939, pet owners thronged to vets' surgeries and animal homes. "Animal charities, the PDSA, the RSPCA and vets were all opposed to the killing of pets and very concerned about people just dumping animals on their doorsteps at the start of the war," says historian Hilda Kean. Battersea Dogs and Cats Home opened its doors in 1860 and survived both wars. "Many people contacted us after the outbreak of war to ask us to euthanise their pets - either because they were going off to war, they were bombed, or they could no longer afford to keep them during rationing," a spokesman says. "Battersea actually advised against taking such drastic measures and our then manager Edward Healey-Tutt wrote to people asking them not to be too hasty." But Campbell cites an Arthur Moss of the RSPCA who, "gloomily pronounced that the primary task for them all would be the destruction of animals".

In the first few days of war, PDSA hospitals and dispensaries were overwhelmed by owners bringing their pets for destruction. PDSA founder Maria Dickin reported: "Our technical officers called upon to perform this unhappy duty will never forget the tragedy of those days."

In Memoriam notices started to appear in the press. "Happy memories of Iola, sweet faithful friend, given sleep September 4th 1939, to be saved suffering during the war. A short but happy life - 2 years, 12 weeks. Forgive us little pal," said one in Tail-Wagger Magazine.

The first bombing of London in September 1940 prompted more pet owners to rush to have their pets destroyed. Many people panicked, but others tried to restore calm. "Putting your pets to sleep is a very tragic decision. Do not take it before it is absolutely necessary," urged Susan Day in the Daily Mirror.

But the government pamphlet had sowed a powerful seed.

"People were basically told to kill their pets and they did. They killed 750,000 of them in the space of a week - it was a real tragedy, a complete disaster," says Christy Campbell, who helped write Bonzo's War. Historian Hilda Kean says that it was just another way of signifying that war had begun. "It was one of things people had to do when the news came - evacuate the children, put up the blackout curtains, kill the cat."

It was the lack of food, not bombs, that posed the biggest threat to wartime pets. There was no food ration allotted for cats and dogs. But many owners were able to make do. Pauline Caton was just five years old at the time and lived in Dagenham. She remembers "queuing up with the family at Black Market in Barking to buy horsemeat to feed the family cat".

And even though there were just four staff at Battersea, the home managed to feed and care for 145,000 dogs during the course of the war. In the middle of the pet-culling mayhem, some people tried desperately to intervene. The

Duchess of Hamilton was one of them - both wealthy and a cat lover - rushed from Scotland to London with her own statement to be broadcast on the BBC. "Homes in the country urgently required for those dogs and cats which must otherwise be left behind to starve to death or be shot." "Being a duchess she had a bit of money and established an animal sanctuary," says historian Kean. The "sanctuary" was a heated aerodrome in Ferne. The duchess sent her staff out to rescue pets from the East End of London. Hundreds and hundreds of animals were taken back initially to her home in St John's Wood. She apologised to the neighbours who complained about the barking.

But at a time of such uncertainty, many pet owners were swayed by the worst-case scenario. "People were worried about the threat of bombing and food shortages, and felt it inappropriate to have the 'luxury' of a pet during wartime," explains Pip Dodd, senior curator at the National Army Museum.

Ultimately, given the unimaginable human suffering that followed over the six years of the war, it is perhaps understandable that the extraordinary cull of pets is not better known. But the episode brought another sadness to people panicked and fearful at the start of war. The story is not more widely known because it was a difficult story to tell. It isn't well known that so many pets were killed because it isn't a nice story, it doesn't fit with this notion of us as a nation of animal lovers. People don't like to remember that at the first sign of war we went out to kill the pussycat.

A Quiet Massacre

When Neville Chamberlain announced that war was declared in 1939, many pet owners dutifully showed up at veterinary clinics and animal shelters to have their pets euthanized. There were reports of lines half a mile long, and of shortages of chloroform, which was the most common veterinary method for euthanasia. A year later, when London was first bombed in September 1940, there would be a second wave of pet owners lining up to have their pets killed. Some of these claimed that they remembered what happened in World War I when starving cats and dogs wandered the streets of London, abandoned, orphaned, and left to suffer deprivation and painful deaths. They wished to prevent their own pets from such needless suffering.

The Opposition

There was opposition to this holocaust. Veterinarians and animal charities such as the PDSA and RSPCA protested that the slaughter of pet animals was unnecessary, inhumane, and an abandonment of British morals. The Army's Veterinary Corp openly worried that many of these dogs who were being killed could well have served a useful military function. Susan Day in the Daily Mirror tried to stem the tide, writing "Putting your pets to sleep is a very tragic decision. Do not take it before it is absolutely necessary." But the pressure was too great and many of the animal shelters reported that their hastily set up euthanasia centers were working around the clock.

One of the oldest animal shelters in Britain is Battersea, which opened its doors in 1860. It survived both world wars and still is in existence today. It did its best to stop the massacre. Even though there were just four full-time staff members at Battersea, the shelter managed to feed and care for 145,000 dogs during the course of the war. In addition, it provided a field in Ilford (East London) where about 500,000 animals were buried, many from the first week of the war.

There was clear governmental duplicity here. Throughout the course of the war, British propaganda would use the German mistreatment of animals as a rallying point. For example, when German ambassador Joachim von Ribbentrop and his staff hastily abandoned their British Embassy they left behind his pet dog (a Chow named Baerchen). This abandonment was widely touted as proof of the Nazi's lack of empathy for animals. An article in the Daily Mirror cited this incident as animal cruelty ran the same day (September 7) that the Times reported that the animal shelters were overflowing with pets brought in to be euthanized because of the government's recommendation.

Why It Is Forgotten

A clear attempt to write this holocaust out of history began during the war. Although the initial advice for people to kill their pets as part of the war effort was never withdrawn, there were no further official publications reiterating that recommendation. Instead, the press began to fill up with stories of civilians killed in bombings alongside their beloved pets or dogs comforting wounded people, and these would be offered as symbols of England's compassion for animals. Photos of military and civil defense personnel rescuing puppies from bombed-out buildings were run prominently, along with commentaries contrasting these humanitarian actions with the indiscriminate evil of the German war machine.

At the beginning of the war, the pet massacre received a lot of attention, but like painful events occurring in a person's life, the memories now seem to be repressed. The historian Hilda Kean reports that when she first approached the archives division of the Royal Society for the Prevention of Cruelty to Animals for information about this slaughter of pets, she was told, via email, "There is no evidence in our surviving records of the time of any 'massacre' of pets at the start of WW2." Kean notes that this statement flies in the face of RSPCA magazine's Animal World report in October 1939 that "the work of destroying animals was continued, day and night, during the first week of the war."

As Freud noted, the first line of defense against something emotionally distressing that is happening now is denial. However, the first line of defense for something that evokes guilt and distress that happened in the past is repression — namely eliminating the event from memory. Although he was talking about individuals, the same mechanisms are used by nations.

Covid-19 Pandemic

With record demand of pet foods during the covid-19 pandemic, shortages of finished product and raw ingredients are developing, alongside increasing prices. Many of the ingredients in the diets below you may already have in your home and will only need to add a few supplements. As with any new food, introduce slowly, be patient, and look at this as an opportunity to introduce diet variations. Concerned your cat may not like your new culinary efforts? Try just the meat initially as a snack and increasingly add to or replace the current diet.

I'll start with a complete and balanced recipe from Dr. Barbara Fougère. You can find the complete recipe and instructions at the link below. Remember, cats need high-protein meat-based diets and do best when fed a variety of meat proteins to prevent monotony. Because cooking destroys essential amino acids, like taurine, cats will benefit more from raw meat. Cats fed cooked food will invariably succumb to nutritional deficiencies. If the foods are cooked, additional amino acids must be added to prevent deficiencies that can lead to health issues. Just as some people do better on some types of diets and foods and not on others, we must recognize each animal is an individual and what works for one may not work for another. It's a good idea to discuss and outline any diet changes with your integrative veterinarian first.

For cats: https://terrigrow.com/basic-recipe-for-cats/
1/3 cup of this diet = ~95 kcal.

Compare to the caloric density on the back of your cat food label. For a 10lb cat, two meals would roughly meet its resting energy requirements of ~190kcals per day. This could vary depending on your cat's weight and activity.

Something Maybe Better Than Nothing

In these challenging times, you may need to either supplement your cat's commercial foods or find there are ingredient shortages for making homemade foof. That's where a walk in the grocery aisles gave me an idea. Foods we often overlook may be just what you need to supplement your cats' foods. While Dr. Fougère's recipes offer some ingredient exchanges, you may still find yourself at a loss. My goal is to help you stretch your resources knowingly. First and foremost, it's important to understand these recommendations are based on "emergency mode: something is better than nothing," and are designed to be used periodically—not long-term—or as healthy snacks. If your cat is on a special diet be sure to discuss it with your integrative veterinarian.

The Finicky Feline

Cats do not choose to be finicky to challenge your patience. A cat's palate is impressive and is designed for survival. There are three things to remember when offering cats new foods:

1) Cats require high protein meat-based diets,
2) They are imprinted with tastes early in life, and
3) They will accept or reject foods based on whether they fulfill their nutritional needs. For example, a cat with thaimine deficiency will refuse fish, even if it usually likes and eats fish.

Therefore, with our emergency mode assignment, we must put on our meat-based glasses to peruse the aisles. Don't forget your commercial canned and dry foods are flavored with platants, so you might have to up your game with flavor enhancers too, such as freeze-dried meat treats. Many companies now offer these treats, but some feline favorites are *Small Batch* and *Whole Life.*

Bravo Cat Treats, and Nature Variety Mixers.

This whole emergency mode idea started when I was shopping and saw the empty meat cases, all except for the dozen or so containers of chicken livers! Now, we can't feed only chicken livers for a cat's meal, but we can sure use it to enhance palatability and liver offers a range of beneficial nutrients. For instance, we can take a pound of ground turkey, add an ounce of chicken liver for a tasty meal. For additional nutrition, add two sardines (packed in water) and mix well. This combo can be used as a meal replacement once or twice a week. In case of a pandemic, stock up on air dried frozen meat powders

Always watch the calorie count. Remember, our goal is to

help offer meal replacements or stretch meal supplies, not to bulk up our feline companions!

While I know there are many recipes and recommendations for using rice or potato with our cats, I prefer to keep carbs close to 5% and adding these types of carbohydrates blows that easily. Even legumes, while low carb, and yes, are used in many commercial foods, must be processed properly and do not offer a complete amino acid profile for obligate carnivores. Used in levels for meal supplements, may set your cat up for problems.

Let's stick to meat-based snacks and food replacements. These are easy to stock up on and work as human and cat food(when balanced properly)

Meat type	Serving	Calories
Canned sardines (w/ bones,packed in water)	2-3 sardines	25kcal/sardine
Canned salmon	2 oz	41kcal/oz
Canned tuna (packed in water)	2 oz	33kcal/oz
Canned mackerel	2 oz or a smear of Anchovy paste	44kcal/oz
Anchovies	2 oz	37kcal/oz
Clams	½ thigh or 1/3 of breast	21kcal/oz
Rotisserie chicken, no spices	1-2 average eggs	67kcal/oz
Scrambled eggs	2 oz	78kcal/egg

Emergency Meal Toppers

Beyond the Practicality

Many of my clients share they are more worried about their pets' food resources, than their own. Hopefully, this information will help alleviate some of that anxiety.

However, I encourage you to look beyond the practicality of adding to the stockpiles of your cats' foods, as you just might find:

You like having better control of the ingredients going into your cat's dish,

You learn and understand more about your cat's nutrition and nutrient needs, and,

You discover a greater appreciation of what goes into our food resources

CHAPTER FOURTEEN

HOW TO SELECT A GOOD COMMERCIAL PET FOOD

Don't buy pet food on advertising alone. Glamorous advertising persuades many pet owners to seek the beautiful vision of a perfect pet food. But do you really look at the label? Do you understand you must read the ingredient panel, not only the front of the bag? It's also critical to question what's behind the label.

Where are the ingredients sourced? Where's the food made and what is the reputation of the manufacturer? Today's pet industry is global and you need to be aware of the benefits and issues that affect the quality of the food you serve.

Buy what's good for your pet, not what you think your pet should eat.

Large volumes of whole grains may be excellent for you, but your cat is a carnivore requiring high levels of meat protein. Fresh vegetables can offer antioxidants and beneficial nutrients, but cats do just fine with minimal amounts. Remember, just because you like the way the label reads, doesn't mean your pet can digest and utilize a particular food. Ingredient variations, cooking temperatures and added supplements all affect the palatability, digestibility and elimination. Chronic digestive issues, skin problems, urinary disorders, and even seizures can be the result of food intolerances.

Grain-Free doesn't necessarily mean high protein or low carb.

Grain Free isn't for every dog or cat. Most pet owners aren't aware grain-free doesn't mean carbohydrate free. In many products, manufacturers simply replace a grain with another starch, one that may be more problematic for your pet. Not to mention, while many grain-frees promote higher protein, they are not all meat as many assume.

Don't buy on price.

The most expensive does not equal the best. For the most part, you get what you pay for in the pet industry, but you must understand what the price tag represents. The most respected foods don't have the balloon advertising and promotional budgets. They spend the money on better quality ingredients, production, and packaging.

Trust me, you've not tried everything.

There are at least 8000 types of pet foods, including dry, canned and raw. Before you say you've tried every food out there for your finicky cat or dog, compare the foods to educate yourself on what you are really feeding. Have you tried something other than dry, considered different proteins or checked for a common ingredient your pet may be intolerant of? Too often, we see a variation of similar products concealed by different brand names.

Don't overfeed.
If you feed dry food it is easy to overfeed due to misinformation about free feeding and the fear of your cat starving. Most dry foods, especially the grain-free versions are packed with calories. Consider it rocket fuel. Understand too, the reason your pet likes the food is because of the flavoring it's coated with, not the stellar ingredients you are enamored by. Overfeeding can result in chronic vomiting, digestive issues, finickiness, and, of course, obesity. Learn your companion's calorie needs for their best body condition.

Holistic veterinarians agree that the very best diet for your animal companion is one that you make yourself.
A homemade diet, carefully balanced nutritionally, and using raw and organic foods, is closest to what Mother Nature intended. However, many of us do not have the resources to make our pets' food, especially for multiple animals. So, for those of us who rely, partially or entirely, on commercial foods for our animals. To make wise selections, the primary tool is the pet food label. It actually provides quite a bit of information.

Here are some guidelines to use in selecting a good-quality diet.

The Name Reveals the Contents

By regulation, the name of a pet food tells us quite a bit about it.

- "Chicken Cat Food" must contain at least 95% chicken (excluding water).
- "Fish and Giblets for Cats" must be 95% fish and giblets together, and there must be more fish than giblets, since fish appears first on the label.

- If the label says "dinner," "platter," "entree," "nuggets," "formula," or similar term, there must be 25% of the named ingredients. That is, "Fish Dinner" must contain 25% fish.
- If more than one ingredient is named, such as "Fish and Giblets Entree," the two together must comprise 25% of the total, and the second ingredient must be at least 3%. A food labeled "Fish and Giblets Entree" may contain anywhere between 13% fish and 12% giblets, to 22% fish and 3% giblets.
- Ingredients labeled as "with" must be present at 3%, such as "Fish Dinner with Giblets."
- An ingredient labeled as a "flavor," such as "Beef Flavor Dinner," may not actually contain beef meat, but more likely will contain beef digest or other beef by-products that give the food a beef flavor.

That said, there are a couple of caveats that you should be aware of:

- It used to be that non-meat ingredients didn't count on the main label, so food labeled "Chicken and Rice Dinner" still had to contain 25% chicken. However, the rules have changed, so now "Chicken and Rice Dinner" could contain 13% chicken and 12% rice and be legally labeled.
- Multiple studies have found many mislabeled pet foods and treats. In some cases, ingredients are present in the food but not disclosed on the label; this is a serious problem if a pet has a food allergy, because the food may contain undeclared allergens. On the other hand, some products contained none of the primary ingredient as stated on the label. The pet food industry and its regulators have no interest whatsoever in fixing the problem.

Watch Out for By-Products

Even on many high-priced, premium, and veterinary brands, you will notice one of the major ingredients listed is "by-products" of some sort. These are basically "parts other than meat." They may include internal organs not commonly eaten by humans, such as lungs, spleens, and intestines, other parts such as cow udders, and in the case of poultry by-products, heads, beaks and feet. By-products must be from "freshly slaughtered" animals, although there is some question as to how fresh they really are by the time they reach the pet food manufacturer, since they may be shipped in unrefrigerated trucks.

By-products(unnamed meat) are usually found in canned foods, where they are often the main or only source of animal protein. While a hunting cat or wild canine would eat the by-products as well as the meat, a named meat should be the mainstay of a carnivore's diet.

What Are Rendered Products?

Rendering (basically a process of slow cooking) produces two major items: animal fat or tallow, and a dry, powdery product usually called "meat meal," "meat and bone meal," or "by-product meal." (Due to historical quirks in naming, the term "by-product meal" refers to poultry, while the equivalent mammal product is "meat and bone meal.")

Animals that are dead, dying, diseased, or disabled prior to reaching the slaughterhouse are known as "downers" or "4D" animals. These are condemned for human consumption, and are typically sent for rendering along with other by-products, parts and items that are unwanted or unsuitable for human use – such as out-of-date supermarket meats, cut-away cancerous tissue, parasitized livers, and fetal tissue (which is very high in hormones).

Rendered ingredients vary greatly in quality. Some rendering facilities are closely associated with slaughterhouses, which are in turn connected with feedlots or poultry farms. These "captive" rendering plants are more likely to produce good quality, relatively pure meals. Such meals are typically designated with the name of the source animal, such as "chicken meal."

Independent renderers may take material from many sources. Many accept such items as road kill, euthanized shelter dogs and cats, and other unappetizing ingredients. These items can be segregated from the food stream, and are not intended for animal food. Renderers can still profit from selling them for use in fertilizers, cosmetics, and industrial applications.

Over the years there have been numerous unsubstantiated reports of this material being processed into dog and cat food. The Center for Veterinary Medicine, a branch of the Food and Drug Administration, long ago admitted that dead dogs and cats are commonly rendered. Although there is no legal prohibition against using dogs and cats in pet food, CVM stated they do not "condone" the practice. Feed cycling within the same species is banned in some states, but feed cycling between species seems to be the loophole pet manufacturers are using to get by legal regulations.

All the large, reputable pet food companies assert that they do not use such materials in their products. But honesty is not always practiced in the pet food industry. Manufacturers must depend on the integrity of their suppliers, which is questionable at best. Research has found that an uncomfortably large number of finished products contain animal proteins that aren't listed on the label. Whether this is through accidental or deliberate contamination isn't known. Not all manufacturers are entirely ethical themselves, either.

Because of the way they are processed, most dry foods use meals as their major animal-source ingredients. "Meals" do contain more protein than whole meat, since the fat and water have been removed. Many dry foods advertise that they contain some type of "meat" (such as chicken or beef) as the first or a top ingredient. However, because of the high water content of fresh meat, and water may also be added to it, the actual percentage of meat protein is tiny. The first named meal is usually the primary protein source in these foods.

What Does "Complete and Balanced" Mean?

A food may be labeled as "complete and balanced" if it meets the standards set by a group called AAFCO, the Association of American Feed Control Officials. Standards set by AAFCO have been adopted by most states; the states are responsible for enforcement.

A food may be certified by AAFCO in two ways:
(1) Meeting published standards for content(Nutrient Profiles) or
(2) Feeding trials.

(1) Nutrient Profiles.

These standards set the required amounts of protein, fat, vitamins, minerals, and so forth. These theoretically have the benefit of extensive research behind them. AAFCO published updated profiles in 2016. But by then, the research was already more than a decade out of date.

Moreover, any manufacturer can synthesize a food containing sufficient amounts of each nutrient according to the standards, yet an animal will ultimately starve to death on it. How could this happen? The standards don't address the"bioavailability" of nutrients. The digestive tract doesn't absorb certain forms of vitamins, minerals, and amino acids. In theory, a food made of old leather boots, wood shavings, and crankcase oil can meet the technical requirements for protein, carbohydrates, and fats, but be completely indigestible.

(2) Feeding Trials.

Many consider this the "gold standard" of pet food formulation. I am not one of them. When you look at the actual AAFCO protocols for an adult maintenance diet, a manufacturer must feed exclusively the test food to only six (out of eight animals) for six months. Kitten and puppy food trials last only 10 weeks. Several of the largest pet food producers, such as Hills, Walthams and Purina, maintain their own colonies of dogs and cats, and test their foods on hundreds of animals over years or even multiple generations.

Other manufacturers rely on testing facilities that keep animals for this purpose to do the studies for them.

It is easy to see how a poor quality diet could be fed for only six months without seeing adverse health effects, yet meet AAFCO standards. Foods that pass feeding trials may still be inadequate for long-term maintenance. Worse still, the AAFCO "family rule" allows the feeding test statement on "similar" foods that were not tested. There are criteria for using that rule, but since there's no way to tell which food actually passed a feeding test, this label designation is all but useless. The standards only set "minimums" and "maximums," not "optimums." Commercial foods are adequate for the average animal, but may not work for an individual animal's variable needs.

Preservatives and Other Additives

Many pet food ingredients can spoil, so manufacturers must add preservatives. BHA, BHT, propyl gallate, propylene glycol (dog food only) and ethoxyquin are all synthetic chemicals. Ethoxyquin is rarely used now, except to preserve fish meal. Contrary to internet lore, even if it's added to an ingredient before reaching the manufacturer, it must be listed on the label.

Contaminants

Pesticides, antibiotics, and molds are common pet food contaminants. Glyphosate, the active component of the herbicide Roundup® is a major contaminant of GMO (genetically engineered) corn and soy. But there is even more glyphosate in many non-GMO crops. Potatoes, legumes, wheat, oats, barley, spinach, and apples are spray-dried with glyphose to make harvesting easier (hence making them cheaper).

Meat from downer animals may be loaded with drugs. Some of them pass unchanged through processing. A toddler who often munched on her cat's dry food died of an allergic reaction to penicillin. The level in the Cat Chow was over 600 times the limit allowed in human food! There have been many major recalls of dry dog food by different manufacturers due to mold contamination of grain ingredients. Some fungal toxins are very dangerous, and have killed more than 120 dogs.

Transitioning to Better Foods

When selecting a commercial food for your animal companion, be sure to read the label. Although percentages are misleading due to the variable moisture content of processed foods, they are often the only data available.

- Pet food makers are clever about marketing. It's important to know how to see through the hype.
- Avoid foods containing "by-product meal," "meat and bone meal," or euphemisms like "beef and bone meal." They tend to be the least expensive (and thus poorest quality) animal-source ingredients. "Meat and bone meal" (MBM) is the mammal equivalent to "[poultry] by-product meal." MBM was reported as the ingredient most likely to contain the drug used for euthanasia (sodium pentobarbital) in a study conducted by the FDA.
- A named meat or meat meal should be the primary protein source. Ingredients like corn gluten meal, pea protein, or by-products are just cheap meat substitutes.
- Stay away from corn and soy. The feed-grade corn and soy in pet food are genetically engineered. Corn gluten meal is often substituted for expensive meat ingredients.
- Never feed "semi-moist" type foods, which are full of additives, colorings, texturizers, flavorings and preservatives.
- Avoid foods containing chemical preservatives. Vitamins C (ascorbic acid), vitamin E (mixed tocopherols) and rosemary or rosemary oil are safer. However, the shelf life of naturally preserved foods is shorter.
- Stay away from "light" or "senior" or "special formula" foods. They may contain inadequate protein, excessive fiber, and poor quality fats that can lead to skin and coat problems or worse.
- Change brands or flavors of dry food every few months.

That way you can avoid deficiencies or excesses of ingredients. It also helps prevent finicky eating behavior.

• Whenever you are changing foods, remember to GO SLOWLY. Add a tiny amount of new food to old, and gradually increase the proportion of new food. It can take weeks to properly transition a cat. Click here for more info on why and how to change foods.

• With canned food, you can change flavors daily if you wish.

• Cats need at least 75% of their diet (ideally 100%!) in the form of wet food (canned, raw, or homemade). Include a variety of meats and flavors to prevent finicky behavior and food allergies and intolerances.

• Do not give dry food to cats who are overweight, diabetic, or have liver issues, pancreatits, urinary problems, or kidney disease. Low moisture and high carbohydrate content contribute to these problems. There is no benefit to the cat from dry food, and many adverse effects on health. Dry food is popular because of its cost and convenience. But it is definitely not healthy for your cat to eat. (And no, dry food does not clean the teeth!)

• If you must feed dry food, do not get it wet, even if the package says it's okay. Do not mix kibble with canned food, milk, broth, or water. All dry foods have bacterial contamination on the surface. Moisture allows those bacteria to grow. Some are harmful and cause vomiting and/or diarrhea.

Make Your Pet's Good Food Even Better!

1. You can safely substitute up to 15% of your pet's total daily food intake as supplemental foods or treats.

2. Add raw (or lightly cooked) meat and organ meats. (Freeze all meat products at -40 F for 72 hours.) Always follow safe meat-handling procedures.
3. Carnivores can't break down plant cell walls, so any plant products (veggies, grains or fruits) must be steamed and/or pureed.
4. Limit all carbohydrates for cats; they're essentially empty calories that only skew glucose metabolism, spike blood sugar and cause weight gain.
5. Other helpful supplements include Omega-3 fatty acids, probiotics such as L. acidophilus (make sure that prebiotic fiber such as psylium is included), digestive enzymes, glandular supplements and antioxidants.

Canned Products

Although balanced raw diets are the most natural, nutritious and beneficial for our cats' health, not everyone is able to embrace the concept at this time. For them, canned food products are the next best option. Because the very nature of cooking changes the proteins and fats that cats depend upon for their energy and health, however, no canned product can truly approach a balanced raw diet in the quality of nutrition it provides and for that reason, this book is strongly pro-raw.

That said...

Choosing Products

The number of canned foods available is absolutely staggering, and the minimal regulation around the manufacture and marketing of these foods allows for some interesting labeling and ingredient sourcing and listing practices. This can cause serious, brow-furrowing confusion for anyone trying to decide what to bring home to their beloved felines.

Important information on choosing canned foods can be found on CatInfo.org's 'Commercial Foods' page. Dr. Pierson goes into extensive detail to help cat owners understand the nutritional composition of canned products and the many ways what you see on the label may vary from what's actually in the can. She also maintains a painstakingly assembled 'Nutritional Composition' chart listing the protein, fat, and carbohydrate percentages of dozens of the most widely available products, and includes an accompanying chart that lists these same products in order of their phosphorus content.

The **TruthAboutPetFood.com** maintains a comprehensive database of products, called Petsumer Report, that rates each product on the quality of the top four or five ingredients. The database requires a small annual fee to access, but includes information the author gleans by calling manufacturing companies directly and red flags potentially toxic and unhealthy ingredients for easy identification – knowledge worth the fee, IMO.

One thing to know right up front – there is no requirement that pet food products receive premarket approval by FDA. In addition, FDA regulations grant fairly wide allowances in naming products. If a product contains any of these, or similar, words: "Dinner," "Platter," "Entree," "Nuggets" or "Formula," then the total of the ingredients named in the title must be greater than 25% but less than 95% of the product on a dry matter basis. Any ingredient proceeded by the word "with" need only comprise 3% DMB of the product.

Products with named ingredients that do not include any of the qualifiers above (for example, "Beef and Chicken Canned Cat Food") must contain at least 95% DMB of the named ingredients – and these are the products that are most likely to provide your cats with the "best" nutritional profiles.

More information on the minimal marketing and labeling regulations can be found on the FDA's Information on Marketing a Pet Food Product page.

The cost of buying for price.

Whether it's pet food or human food, veterinary services or your medical care, or an accessory for you or your pet, are you aware of the cause and affect you initiate when buying on price alone?

Every day stores compete for your business. Products and goods can be found for a range of prices, yet many of us do not think about the loss or gains beyond our own wallet.

With the growth in the pet industry over the last 15 years, we—pet owners—have been subject to a range of cause and effects of buying for price and all too often ignorant of the cost of that good deal.

From a health perspective, how did we get to the point we can feed our pets for pennies? Quality foods are an investment—an investment in your companion animal and an investment in the companies who take on the responsibility of nourishing your companion. Cheap, abundant ingredients are available but at a cost to your companion, knowledgeable and ethical businesses, and reliable suppliers.

The pet food recall of 2007 was a major turning point in the pet food industry. Pet owners, incensed with betrayal, blamed manufacturers and exporters while searching for something better. New natural food brands exploded on the market and natural pet stores began popping up like dandelions. But "better" comes at a price and pet owners hailed discount sources greedily. Why not? You can have that preferred recommended brand your dependable local natural store spent time educating you on, at a bargain. Multiply that a 100 times or tens of thousands. Without the revenue support of loyal customers, will that local, resourceful store be able to help you down the road? What about the manufacturer, who opted to reach a larger number of clients through mass marketers, only to find themselves working harder for less profit? Can that manufacturer maintain cutting edge research and premium quality ingredients with less funding?

Understand too these "better" foods will reflect ingredient, transportation and manufacturing increases. If not and you find the food at a bargain price, ask yourself at what cost? If that brand is cheaper, what did the manufacturer, distributor or retailer take advantage of to make it less expensive? Cheaper ingredients, cheap labor, or something we are starting to see more of: the manipulation of power and greed. The behind the scenes business side of the pet industry are beginning to resemble the hoarders the humane organizations fight against. The difference, instead of animals, it's about hoarding the market.

Make no mistake, I am all for capitalism and the freedom of choice of where I spend my dollar. But, we must ask ourselves when clicking that "Buy" button, what is the true cost to us and our companions?

The thing is, the best pet food cannot be found in a bag or can. Yet, the pet industry has convinced you and your veterinarian that proper nutrition can only be found from commercial sources. Think about your options the next time you reach for that heavily promoted super premium food. Do you know where the meat protein of that food was sourced? Is the cannery ethical? Has the kibble manufacturer followed all food safety protocols?

These are questions your community pet store should be on top of and it takes your support to make sure they can be there for you. Think about that the next time you need help with your companion and how you invested your money.

CHAPTER FIFTEEN

WHOLE BONE ALTERNATIVES: WHEN AND HOW TO USE THEM IN A RAW FED CAT'S DIET

As discussed in the article, 'Dem Bones, 'Dem Bones, 'Dem... Scary Bones', there is no true substitute for fresh, whole bone-in meals in a raw fed cat's diet. It's not just about nutrition – chomping and crunching those pliable bones are extremely important for dental, digestive, and mental health.

What we ideally attempt to create when feeding raw is a food modeled on the perfect food for a cat – a mouse, rat, or rabbit. And mice, rats, and rabbits have bones from which our kitties derive many needed minerals, trace elements and other nutrients – not just calcium. And it's a given that nutrients are best consumed in their natural, unprocessed form. Not only can processing damage them, but our increasing knowledge in the field of nutrition includes a broader understanding of the complex, synergistic nature of many nutrients, and the health benefits of consuming them in the same combinations and ratios as they naturally occur. The importance of providing nutrients in as natural a form as possible cannot be stressed enough; the more we deviate from that natural model, the more likely we are to be providing a less-than-optimal nutrient profile.

This highlights one of the biggest advantages of creating our own cat food over purchasing commercially processed products; we can control the extent to which nutrients are provided in their natural form. The closer we come to that objective – the closer we are to actually recreating a mouse – the less nutritional unknowns are a factor. The ability to tailor the diet to specific needs is another important advantage of creating our own cat food.

As important as it is to mimic the natural, there are times, in this less than ideal world, when we need a whole raw bone alternative, such as:

1. Transitioning to prey model raw
2. Cats with no teeth or dental problems
3. Cats with special medical needs, such as kidney disease / chronic renal failure
4. Cats with impaired GI systems that make digesting and metabolizing whole bone difficult (at least initially).
5. Kittens (2-4 weeks old) without milk teeth.

Alternatives to fresh, whole bones for raw feeders include:

– Ground bone

– Fresh bone alternatives:
– Freeze-dried bone: Microcrystalline Calcium Hydroxyapatite (MCHA)
– Eggshells (97% calcium carbonate)
– Bone meal

Ground Bone

As close to natural as possible without being whole, feeding ground food is the first and best of your options. Due to the potential for oxidation of nutrients, however, ground food must be at least minimally supplemented. There are several time-tested recipes for ground food available, notably at Dr. Lisa Pierson's of CatInfo.org and that of Anne Jablonsky of CatNutrition.org.

Fresh Bone Alternatives

Eggshells

In some cases, such as the need to lower phosphorus intake in cats with kidney failure, eggshells can be substituted entirely for bone. (There are other sources of calcium carbonate, including limestone and oyster shells, but eggshells are a far superior option and the only one discussed herein.)

Each type of fowl produces shells with slightly varying composition (and, as with all raw diets, rotation – even of your eggshell sources – is encouraged!). Obviously the diet of the chicken, duck, quail, etc. has an impact on the shell composition, particularly as regards trace minerals. That said, eggshells are an excellent bone substitute, as they are composed of similar minerals as bone, only with significantly less phosphorus and sodium. This is what makes eggs the perfect bone substitute for cats requiring a low phosphorus diet, e.g. cats with kidney disease (CKD) or in chronic renal failure (CRF).

Analysis of eggshells from varying breeds of chicken, duck and quail from around the world find underlying similarities – the primary mineral is calcium carbonate (ranging from 84% in quail eggs to 97% in chicken eggs), followed by small amounts of magnesium (from 0.2% in duck eggs, to 0.3% – 0.4% in chicken eggs), and trace amounts of sodium, potassium, zinc, manganese, iron, copper, boron, chromium, selenium, and vanadium.

A Special Note on Using Eggshell Powder for Cats with Special Medical Needs, Specifically Kidney Disease or Chronic Renal Failure

Although restricting the phosphorus content in foods for kitties suffering from CKD/CRF has been shown in studies to be very beneficial in protecting the kidney from further damage, it can be done without lowering the protein content (as was once the recommendation). And new studies have shown maintaining a high protein diet is crucial to the ongoing health of the cat.

A typical prey model raw meal is ~ 2.0% phosphorus on a dry matter basis. The prescription CKD/CRF foods target 0.5% phosphorus on a dry matter basis. Modifying a prey model raw diet (whether fed in PMR format or ground) by substituting eggshell for bone, the phosphorus load is reduced to about 0.8% on a dry matter basis. Depending on kitty's kidney function, that switch to eggshell from bone may be more than sufficient to reduce the load on the kidneys to healthy function. The diet remains high in the B-vitamins that would otherwise need to be supplemented, and provides the high level of protein your cat needs to prevent muscle wasting. If this move alone does not help control the phosphorus excretion, up to 10% of the diet can be substituted with egg whites, raw or cooked.

Egg whites provide high protein with NO phosphorus. This brings the phosphorus in the diet down to approximately the 0.5% (dry matter basis) targeted by the prescription diets, yet provides the cat with a species-appropriate diet that is easily digestible and highly bioavailable – a far cry from highly processed prescription kibble and canned products. The high moisture in this diet also helps keep kitty hydrated and all her organs (including those kidneys!) well lubricated.

For an excellent overview of feline kidney disease, please see Tanya's Comprehensive Guide to Feline Chronic Kidney Disease: http://www.felinecrf.org/

How to Make Eggshell Powder

The best eggshells to use are those from organically, naturally raised, pastured animals. (In the U.S. "free range" does not mean they have access to a pasture.) You can see the difference in the yolk. In locally raised, pastured chickens, the yolk is a deep orange color. Compare this to the pale yellow yolks of regular supermarket eggs. With traditional supermarket eggs, your cat will be getting the calcium she needs, but not the same range of trace minerals.

If you eat (or feed) eggs, providing eggshell powder to your cat is easy and economical. Save the shells, rinse away any remaining white. Keep the membrane (it provides glucosamine and chondroitin, good for joint health). Dry them: Place them on a plate in the hot sun for a few days to a week, or place them in the oven at 300 Degrees for 10 or

15 minutes, or bake them at 200 degres for 30 minutes. Tip: Put the shells in the oven to dry when you're preheating to bake something else, or after you've cooked something on high heat.

When the shells are brittle and crumbly to the touch, they're ready for the (clean) coffee grinder. You'll likely have to "pulse" it several times. The goal is to grind them as finely as possible, the approximate consistency of baking powder. Let them rest in the grinder for 15 or 20 minutes before opening it or you'll have a cloud of eggshell dust puff out. Store the eggshell powder in an air-tight glass jar so it remains dry. One medium-large egg will produce roughly one teaspoon of eggshell powder.

Summary

In conclusion, there are several options when it becomes necessary to modify the whole bone content of your raw-fed cat's diet, including replacing it altogether. So whether you're transitioning a GI-compromised cat that can't yet handle whole bone, dealing with a toothless kitty, or adjusting for a recently received CRF diagnosis, feeding your beloved feline the foods she's meant to eat – the most nutritious and easily digestible diet possible – is within reach.

References

1. Dr. Peter Hunton, Calcium Sources for Laying Hens, Poultry Industry Council of Canada, Factsheet #133.
2. Know What You Feed: FAQ
3. This database is updated periodically. As of the writing of this article, the current release is SR25, September 2012.
4. NutritionData.com, Nutritional Effects of Food

Processing.

5. Butcher, GD and Miles RD. Concepts of Eggshell Quality, Poultry Science Department, University of Florida, Gainesville, pub Alachua Free Network (AFN.org).; Shen, TF and Chen WL 2003. The Role of Magnesium and Calcium in Eggshell Formation in Tsaiya Ducks and Leghorn Hens, Asian-Aust J. Anim. Sci. 16(2): 290-296.

6. Thanks to Holisticat for the discussion on the use of eggshell as bone substitute.

8. Brigham and Women's Hospital Encyclopedia.

CHAPTER SIXTEEN

Starting Kittens on Raw Diets

Kittens are the most amenable of all cat lifestages to take to raw. The best food for just born kittens is mom's milk. Kittens typically start getting their milk teeth, also known as deciduous or baby teeth, around 2 to 4 weeks of age. The incisors (front teeth) are the first to emerge, followed by the canines (pointy teeth) around 3 to 4 weeks. By the time they are 4 to 6 weeks old, the premolars (located behind the canines) also appear and this is a good time to start introducing raw food. In the wild, mama cats eat and reguritate the prey animal for kittens. We mimic that by giving ground up or chopped finely to assist eating.

What to feed a kitten who doesn't have milk teeth yet

Lots of mama cats go missing in action after birthing their litter. Some get killed by dogs or meet with an untimely death. This doesn't bode well for the just born litter who are very dependant on their mom for feeding, pooping and warmth. You might have to get a baby feeding bottle and get ready to be a full-time mom for such kittens. Kittens feed 5-6 times a day and need to be stimulated to poop. The best option is to find a lactating mom cat and add the orphan kittens to her brood. Most mama cats don't differentiate.

I looked up some popular Kitten Milk Replacement brands. The ingredients made me cringe. But I went to the blackboard and started making a list of all available whole ingredients that could resemble cat's milk: liver, raw goats/ camel milk, diluted cow raw milk, egg yolks etc.

Cow Milk: High in protein, fat, and lactose. Rich in calcium and vitamin D.

Goat Milk: Slightly higher in calories and fat than cow milk. Lower in lactose, making it easier to digest for cats.

Camel Milk: Lower in fat and lactose compared to cow and goat milk. Rich in vitamins and minerals, especially vitamin C.

Cat Milk: High in calories, protein, and fat. Lower in lactose, similar to camel milk.

Each type of milk has its unique nutritional profile and benefits. For example, camel milk is often preferred by those with lactose intolerance due to its lower lactose content, while goat milk is known for being easier to digest than cow milk.If you can get camel's milk, get it, it has a similar lactose content as cat's milk.

Here are some homemade kitten milk replacement formula recipes that include colostrum powder, egg yolk, goat or camel milk, liver, and bone broth:

Recipe 1: Goat Milk and Colostrum Formula

Ingredients:

1 quart whole raw goat's milk/camel milk

1 teaspoon light Karo syrup/Molasses/ Raw Brown Sugar(don't use honey)

1 tablespoon plain yogurt (preferably made with goat's milk or raw cow milk)

1 egg yolk(chicken or duck)

1 teaspoon colostrum powder

2-3 raw liver (finely chopped or blended)

20 ml bone broth

Instructions:

Put the goat's milk in a saucepan and warm it till lukewarm(never boil raw milk), and add the appropriate amount of bone broth based on the kitten's age.

Mix in the remaining ingredients, including the colostrum powder, raw liver, and egg yolk in a blender or mixie.

Strain, Put in feeding bottles abd feed immediately. Refrigerate the leftovers. It will keep up to two days in the refridgerator and upto a week frozen.

You can freeze dry the leftovers and make instant KMR by adding an equal portion of water.

Weaning Kittens to Raw

Weaning kittens onto raw is the best way to give a good start to life to your kittens. Not only is their development better, but their immune system is healthier among many other benefits that will only continue into adulthood if raw feeding is continued. Here is the simple way to wean kittens on to raw. Keep in mind that most often when mom is already on raw, kittens very quickly take to raw as they watch what their mother is doing and eating.

Some raw feeders do not recommend any kind of milks (KMR, goats milk etc.) nor pro/prebiotics (unless absolutely necessary) to kitten in order to give them a chance to build their gut flora naturally. They have the advantage of not being compromised by commercial pet foods and kitten milk replacement formulas which affect the natural microflora.

A kitten eating a rabbit

For orphans or kittens being hand-reared please skip to the end of this section. Their transition will be different than those weaning straight from mom.

Weaning from mom:

If I start seeing interest from the kittens to mom's food, at 3-4 weeks I add some home prepared ground complete meals in with my queen's food so they have something to nibble on.

Around 4-5 weeks I begin adding small chunks to the ground mixture.

Between 5-8 weeks I add larger and larger chunks until they can start chewing bone.

By 8 weeks they are eating big chunks of meat about 1" or so in size as well as bone like chicken necks, rabbit ribs, small prey like mice. During this whole time span I provide as much variety in protein source as I can. Rotate between chicken, beef, mutton, quail, turkey and rabbit if you can afford it(or atleast 3-4 from the 6 meals listed, at least)

Recap:

Age 3-4 weeks

Offer ground complete meal with mother's meals

4-5 weeks

Small chunks with the ground mix

5-8 weeks

Increase the size of chunks and start adding whole bone(not ground)

8 weeks

Eating big chunks of meat and bone like chicken necks, rabbit ribs and whole prey

Kittens are usually fed at least 3-4 times a day as much as they want per sitting within reason (we don't want them vomiting from eating too much at one time.) If they are hungry more throughout the day we give more feedings.

8 weeks+=Good to go for the rest of their lives....

Weaning orphaned or hand rearing kittens

Unfortunately some kittens are unable to stay with mum and need hand rearing. Weaning these little ones to raw is slightly different as they don't have mum to copy or eat from.

I start the raw weaning at 3 weeks of age. I start on a flat plate. Kittens can eat as much as they want over 4-6 sittings a day. It is best to feed them before their milk replacement (KMR), if you are giving any.

At three weeks old I offer ground tripe or ground skinless boneless chicken. Kittens usually become interested in food between 3-4 weeks old. As kittens learn from their mother's sometimes you will need to encourage eating. You can do this by rubbing a small bit of the ground tripe or chicken on their nose (not blocking their nostrils) for them to lick off.

At four weeks I then start adding in some ground chicken bone at 10% of the mix (wings work best) into the tripe or chicken mix. Once bone is added over the next few days slowly start to introduce some different ground proteins at increments of 2-3 days.

At 5 weeks you can start adding the liver and offal slowly. Whilst doing this begin to offer small pieces of meat into the ground meat and bone mix. When they are eating the small chunks you can make the pieces bigger.

At 6 weeks they should be on the 80/10/10 with ground bone and small to medium chunks of meat and offal. At this stage you can offer bigger chunks of meat and begin to offer chunks of bone. It is best to get some chicken wings and bash them with a hammer (beware of sharp edges). Continue feeding small pieces of wing through the week. By the end of week six they should be on medium chunks of meat and offal and small pieces of bone.

At 7 weeks you can start to offer larger pieces of bone and meat. Throughout this week slowly make the bone pieces bigger until you are offering whole wings or wing tips. At the same time making the meat chunks bigger to large pieces.

At 8 weeks they should now be on whole bone and medium to large chunks of meat and offal. You can now offer different soft bones like necks. During week 8 offer various bone choices.

At 9 weeks they should now be ready for their new homes and able to eat medium to large pieces of meat and bone. They can now continue their raw journeys in their new homes .

RECAP:
Week 3:
Ground tripe or chicken.
Week 4:
Add ground bone and other ground proteins
Week 5:
Add liver and offal. Add small meat chunks to the ground meat.
Week 6:
Add bigger chunks of meat and small chunks of bone.
Week 7:
Add larger bone pieces working towards whole bone.
Week 8:
Whole bone and medium to large chunks of meat. Start adding different whole bones.
Week 9:
Fully weaned and ready to go.

PREY MODEL RAW (PMR) Diet for Kittens

The Prey Model Raw (PMR) diet eliminates processed foods and provides kittens with a natural diet which mimics what their ancestors and wild cousins consumed. A complete PMR diet mimics whole, wild prey animals and does not include plant ingredients.

The PMR diet is one of the many raw diet types suitable for kittens. It is important to note that many ratio raw diets can be lacking in certain essential nutrients when specific whole foods are not fed. Ratio diets are a great base and adding several additional whole foods can help to fill the common nutritional gaps.

Prey Model Raw (PMR)

The recommended guidelines for a kitten PMR diet is 64-69% muscle meat, 17% raw edible bone, 7% liver, and 7% other secreting organs, and 0-5% animal based fiber. Franken Prey is another term used for raw feeders who follow PMR ratio guidelines but do not feed whole, intact prey animals.

Instead of whole prey, a variety of animal ingredients are used to complete PMR ratio guidelines. Meals can consist of multiple protein sources and different ingredients in a single feeding. It is important to note that most PMR diets are not able to mimic wild prey completely. Therefore, additional whole foods or supplements are frequently necessary to fill the common nutritional gaps.

64-69 PERCENT(Muscle Meat)

PMR diets consist of raw muscle meat to provide essential protein, amino acids, and water-soluble vitamins. The muscle meat ratio guideline starts at 64-69% of the overall daily intake.

It is important to note the muscle meat ratio does not mean to feed muscle meat exclusively. This ratio is a large category containing multiple ingredients including saturated fat for energy and muscular organs such as heart and tripe.

17 PERCENT(Raw Edible Bone)

Soft, raw edible bones are an important component in PMR diets for kittens to provide essential calcium, phosphorus, and other essential nutrients. Kittens have higher calcium and phosphorus requirements than adult cats. Therefore, the kitten PMR diet has a higher edible bone percentage. The raw edible bone ratio guideline starts at 17% of the overall daily intake.

It is important to note that this ratio refers to the amount of bone alone, and does not include the meat on the bone. Since various raw meaty bones will differ in their bone content, some calculations will be required to know how much of each raw meaty bone to feed.

The amount of raw meaty bones a kitten may need to maintain firm and consistent stool will vary. The 17% edible bone ratio is a starting guideline. Many kittens do well on 15% to 20% raw edible bone content. Always adjust according to the kitten's individual needs.

High Calcium Requirements for Development

Kittens have a much higher requirement for calcium per 1000kcal in comparison to adult cats. Therefore PMR diets require a higher percentage of edible bone to provide sufficient amounts of calcium for healthy growth and development. The amount of edible bone decreases significantly once the kitten is no longer growing. You can add a teaspoon or a pinch or eggshell powder for added calcium.

7 PERCENT Liver

Liver is an important ingredient in PMR diets for puppies as it provides essential fat-soluble vitamin A and water-soluble vitamins. Ruminant liver also provides the essential mineral copper. The liver ratio guideline is slightly higher in kitten PMR diets due to their higher need for essential nutrients during optimal growth. Liver ratio guideline starts at 7% of the overall daily intake.

The 6% liver ratio is a starting guideline and this amount of liver provides more than recommended allowances for vitamin A. For kittens who are sensitive to organs, feeding as low as 5% liver will still provide essential vitamin A. It is recommended to include ruminant liver such as beef or lamb liver in raw diets for kittens.

7 PERCENT -Other Organs

Other secreting organs, particularly spleen, are beneficial ingredients in PMR diets for kittens to provide essential minerals and water-soluble vitamins. Similar to the liver ratio, the other organ ratio guideline starts at 7% of the overall daily intake.

Other secreting organs are beneficial in completing essential nutrient requirements for kittens. The 6% ratio guideline is a starting recommendation, and more or less, a secreting organ can be fed to complete nutritional requirements.

.5 PERCENT Animal-Based Insoluble Fiber

PMR ratio guidelines fail to include fiber-based foods, which would be present in true whole prey feeding. Therefore, including an animal-based fiber source to Franken Prey feeding methods is recommended. Foods that include fur or feathers provide insoluble fiber to the diet to promote colon health.

Traditional PMR ratios do not provide an animal-based fiber ratio guideline. However, 2 to 5% by weight of "furry" or "feathered" ingredients is a good recommendation to include in daily meals. This will help provide 1-2% fiber in the diet. Be sure to account for any bone and meat that is also provided by the furry ingredients.

It is important to note that the 2-5% ratio refers to the furry ingredients as a whole, which will also include the skin and tissue in the weight. Do not feed the weight in fur or feathers alone. Appropriate sources of fur can include: rabbit feet, rabbit ears, rabbit heads, feathered poultry heads or legs, raw or safely dried animal skin with fur.

When furry or feathered ingredients are not accessible, it is recommended to include a plant fiber source such as psyllium husk in PMR diets at 1.25 tsp per pound of food.

Nutritional Deficiencies

If a PMR diet is fed without specific raw ingredients, the raw diet will be deficient in a few essential nutrients. The ratio guidelines for a PMR diet for kittens are category terms and may include a variety of ingredients that provide different nutrients essential to a kitten's health.

CLOSING COMMENTS

Kitten Prey Model Raw (PMR) ratios are different than adult cat PMR ratios since kittens have higher requirements for certain essential nutrients. PMR diets for kittens do not include plant ingredients because kittens and cats are obligate carnivores. Kittens have requirements for essential nutrients. The diet must supply the nutrients in adequate amounts to be considered balanced.

How Do I Feed My Kitten A Balanced Raw Diet?

Congratulations! COVID-19 has inspired many people to invite pets into their homes. Cats have a wonderful way of making us smile and they can be real comedians at times. But taking on a kitten is a real responsibility and there is an overwhelming amount of information out the about how to care for them

Can I Feed My Kitten A Raw Diet? - YES!

At RDBK, we believe that feeding fresh food to kittens from an early age is imperative for health and longevity. Due to the adorable and fluffy nature of kittens, we sometimes forget that they are highly specialized carnivores that require their nutritional needs to be addressed in a very particular way. In order to prevent disease and give young cats the best chance at health and longevity, we need to honour their true carnivorous nature.

Preventable Diseases

The Banfield Veterinary State of Pet Health report indicates that the most common diseases affecting modern felines are obesity, diabetes, osteoarthritis, kidney disease and dental disease. All of these problems are directly linked to diet. To avoid these illnesses, we need to feed cats in a way that allows them to keep themselves healthy. Processed foods tend to work against them in this regard.

What Is An Obligate Carnivore?

Felines belong to a group called the obligate carnivores. This means that they need a meat-based diet to survive. There is no such thing as a vegetarian diet for cats. While the pet food industry acknowledges that cats need meat, things have gotten pretty off-track when it comes to creating diets that resemble what they would eat in nature. Cats are also considered a partially domesticated species. This means they are able to leave our care and go off on their own to hunt for themselves to survive. But modern processed cat diets are filled with low quality meat, starchy carbohydrates and other highly inappropriate ingredients. And yes, even the "grain-free" processed foods can create problems.

In order to keep your kittens and cats in the best health, we can't forget that these cute balls of fluff are a specialized species with the same needs as other obligate carnivores. I have spent many years working with wild cats but the secret is..... I actually use this experience and education to feed domestic cats as well. And the results are pretty incredible. Cats are a really self-sufficient species when they are given access to appropriate nutrition.

Studies Reflect These Findings As Well!

Studies show significantly better digestibility of raw diets over processed feeds and pave the way for a healthier microbiome in cats.

There Is A Myth Going Around About Fresh Food Diets...

We've been hearing from a lot of new kitten parents that have been told not to feed fresh food because it will cause nutritional deficiencies. While it's possible for nutrient deficiencies to occur..... it's not very common. And it can be easily avoided! I have been feeding kittens and cats fresh food for over 20 years with no developmental issues. In fact, my own cats and my client's cats thrive on species-appropriate raw foods. There are just a few simple guidelines you need to stick to if you want to do it right.

How To Balance Your Kittens Raw Diet

Here is a list of "easy-to-digest" rules to stick to for your kitten's diet:

1. Variety As some of you may have heard or experienced, cats can be very picky! And this starts in kittenhood. Starting your kitten off with a varied raw diet full of different meats, organs and other foods sets them up to be way less picky with food as adults. Switching young cats is much easier than switching older cats who are stuck on the processed food train. Just like people, it can be hard for them to change their habits. Starting young is the best time to get them interested in fresh food!

Additionally, by ensuring enough variety in your kittens diet, you also ensure your kitten gets enough other minerals like potassium, iron, magnesium, zinc, etc, be sure to use a variety of other proteins, organs and bones. Eg. chicken , beef, lamb, goat, turkey,mutton, quail, pork etc.

2. Calcium

The number one source of calcium in the raw diet is raw bone. Feed poultry or rabbit with ground bone at least 4 days per week. It is easy to maintain the calcium levels in your kitten's diet this way. Unlike people, cats have to ability to digest bone and utilize the minerals from it. So, if you're providing enough ground bone, you'll be doing great.

3. Mineral Supplements

If your kitten has GI (gastrointestinal) issues or suspected allergies and cannot eat bones or raw meat, you will need to use a mineral supplement. The best option is steamed food grade bone meal powder. In a pinch, eggshell powder can be used. Dosage for bone meal and egg shell powder: 1.5% of the total meat portion of your kitten's meal. You cannot go wrong with adding a pinch on meals.

4. Sufficient Fat Content

Your kitten needs energy from fat so, whichever raw diet(s) you choose, the nutrition analysis should be, on average, between 8-11% fat, although kittens can do with higher fat content(up to 20%) becuase of their growing body.

5. Omega 3's

Add an omega 3 supplement to the diet. Our favourites: krill oil, canned sardines (packed in water) and marine phytoplankton.

6. Taurine

Cats have a specific need for the amino acid taurine since their bodies cannot make it from other nutrients. This means that you need to pay special attention to your kitten's daily taurine intake. Poultry is adequate in taurine eg. chicken and turkey. But.... If your cat can't or won't eat these, you'll need to add a supplement. Be sure to add 250 mg of free form taurine to your cat's daily meal schedule with non-poultry meals.

7. **Probiotics**

Optimize the diet by including probiotics for healthy gut and immune development. Probiotics don't always have to come from a bottle. Natural ingredients are brimming with gut-flora boosting enzymes essential for a young kitten -

gizzard, tripe, a spponful of raw cow's milk on meals, sliced livers and secreting organs.

A load of poo

Ok, so hopefully after getting this far, you won't think this book is a load of poo. Poo is a great indication of knowing that we are getting it right.

If you have a hard white crumbly poo, this is an indication that you are feeding too much bone, on the other hand, if you get a runny poo, you could be feeding too much offal.

Use your cats poo to use as a guideline.

Yes, that's right, poop can be a great indicator of health! It's also a useful way to tell whether or not you're feeding too much or too little bone. Indoor felines tend to be more on the constipated side so it's important to keep an eye on the litter box habits. Stool that is light in colour, dry or crumbly or hard to pass indicates you are feeding too much bone, especially if this is happening every day. Stools that are dark in colour and soft on a regular basis indicates that you may not be feeding enough bone. Poops should vary in colour, depending on what you are feeding that day. Don't be surprised to see differences in stool colour and formation as they eat different foods. That is totally normal! Just be sure that stools are moist, firm but not hard and easy to pass.

Raw Feeding Cats – Transition Guide

Cats, are obligate carnivores which means they are strict meat eaters, they need meat to survive. Commercial wet cat foods contain as little as 4% meat (which is actually meat derivatives and the company probably cannot tell you what animal the meat derivatives come from).

Kittens are easy to get transitioned onto a raw diet – it's pretty impossible to overfeed a kitten. Kittens have a high activity level and therefore they use of a lot of energy which then means they need lots of food to replace this. You should feed a kitten as much as it will eat over a number of different meal times. If your kitten is less active then you will need to feed less.

Changing cats to a raw diet can take time. A lot of perseverance and patience is needed with the majority of cats. However, you could be very lucky and your cat will eat a raw bit of chicken straight away (or perhaps has stolen some from the dogs bowl).

Transitioning a cat to raw is completely different to transitioning a dog, a dog will eat when he is hungry, therefore you can fast until he eats what has been put in front of him.

With cats you CANNOT fast them, do not go cold turkey, tough love is absolutely not an option! Cats have to eat otherwise they will start breaking down their own body protein – this is dangerous so please take the time to read below on transitioning and be prepared to have some patience – it will be worth it in the end!

What are you feeding now?

24 hour kibble buffet? If you have an all you can eat 24 hour buffet the first step you will need to take is to stop the buffet and have set meal times.

This does not necessarily mean you should stop feeding kibble altogether at this current moment, instead this means that you should let your cat have limited access to the bowl at set times/ timescales per day, this will make the switch easier as your cat will have times when he is hungry.

P.S: Oftentimes, kittens take to raw straight away, then you don't need to follow these steps!

Once you have got the meal times sorted, the next step would be to gradually get your cat switched to eating a high quality wet food. Again, this can take time so please be patient!

The reasoning behind this is because kibble and raw are completely different textures, so changing to something with a similar texture will make the change to raw a bit easier once your cat is fully fed on wet food.

A mixture of kibble & wet?

If you were feeding a mixture of kibble and wet originally, then you can just ditch the kibble altogether and just feed the wet. If you are just feeding kibble, then it is best to introduce the wet food slowly by adding a little bit at a time, decreasing the kibble and increasing the amount gradually over time until your cat is on 100% raw food!

This is a general guideline, so please listen to your cat, every cat is different, what works for one may not work for the other!

Wet food? The next step would be to now start adding little bits of raw to your cats wet food. Gradually increase the raw and reduce the wet until your cat is 100% on raw. However, cats can be incredibly fussy and again this may take time! You may have to become an expert in disguising bits of raw into the wet. It has been known that some cats do not recognise raw as food because it is less fragrant than wet/ kibble. You may have to entice them by adding some bone broth to the mix, or sprinkling crushed kibble on top.

If they still aren't eating the raw, another idea would be to add boiled chicken to the wet and gradually reduce the boiling time until it's raw and then increase the amount of raw chicken and reduce the wet. Also, some cats do not like eating from a bowl, try using a plate with chunks of meat spread apart over the plate.

REMEMBER: Slow and steady wins the race Once your cat has fully made the switch there are a few bits you will need to know about getting the balance correct.

What can I feed?

The diet should be made up of 80% meat 10% bone and 10% offal (5% must be liver). Both of my cats enjoy chicken wings, duck necks, chicken necks, chicken carcass, lamb ribs and if you are feeling brave they also have whole prey such as day old chicks and day old ducklings.

They can have lots of different proteins, my cats genuinely have what I can get my hands on – chicken, beef, lamb, duck, kangaroo, goat, rabbit, pheasant, pigeon, partridge, poussin, oily fish, venison, to name just a few, they also have raw eggs.

REMEMBER: slow introductions are key when introducing new meats and lots of variety.

Taurine

There are only 2 major differences when it comes to feeding cats raw. The first one is that there is no need to feed fruit or veg and secondly, cats need taurine in their daily diet in order to survive.

Taurine is a type of amino acid. Amino acids form the main constituents of all proteins. Taurine is exclusively found in animal-based proteins. It is critical for vision, digestion, heart muscle function, and to maintain a healthy immune system. Taurine is an essential amino acid in the cat.

How will I ensure my cat is getting enough Taurine? I would just like to make it clear that you can never overdo it when it comes to taurine and cats. What taurine is not needed by the body will be passed in the urine.

Taurine is found in darker, harder working muscle meats such as heart (which contains the most taurine) and thigh meats (turkey, chicken), so just make sure you are feeding enough of these meats. Rabbit contains the lowest taurine content but is the leanest meat. Pork contains thaimine.

Mincing meat reduces the taurine amount because the amino acids are open to bacteria which destroys the taurine amount present. Chunks of meat contain more taurine as less of the surface area is open to bacteria.

How much do I feed?

Again, every cat is different and you will need to take into consideration your cats activity level, age, weight but general guidelines are to feed about 3-5% of your cats body weight. If your cat is overweight you will need to reduce this accordingly.

CHAPTER SEVENTEEN

Eight Strikes Against Feeding Fish To Cats

This chapter will count eight distinct reasons against the idea of regularly feeding fish, raw or cooked, to cats.

Strike One: Low calcium levels.
Whole fish, even with bone, is far too low in calcium for a cat. Remember: if you're making homemade cat food, one of the most important things to get right is the ratio of calcium to phosphorus. You have some wiggle room here, but not much. A whole ground fish would be low in calcium. And while the high phosphorus is not good for any cat, elevated phosphorus levels are something you most definitely wouldn't want to feed a cat that is suffering from any kind of kidney problem.

Strike Two: Thiamin destruction.
Raw fish contains high amounts of an enzyme called thiaminase–an enzyme that destroys Vitamin B-1 (thiamin). A thiamin-deficient diet can lead to neurological problems and seizures in cats. Not good.

Strike Three: Urinary tract problems.

Fish, with its high magnesium content, can contribute to a type of urinary tract problem in cats.

Curiously, the discovery some time back of magnesium as a culprit in feline urinary tract disorders was accompanied by the development of specialized 'urinary tract' formula foods. The idea with these foods was to add acid to the food, reasoning that magnesium crystals develop in alkaline, not acid urine. The problem is, cats whose urinary tract acid is too high are prone to another type of crystal–calcium oxylate. Just another reason it's best to feed a cat a diet that nature intended. As Dr. Elizabeth Hodgkins points out in her book, the rise of urinary tract diseases in the cat coincided exactly with the increasing use of dry kibble to feed cats.

Strike Four: Addiction.

Heaven knows, most cats absolutely adore the taste of fish. Anyone who's ever opened up a can of fish within a 12-city-block radius of any hungry feline knows that. But you can quickly end up with a 'fish addict' on your hands. And the last thing you need is a cat on a hunger strike refusing to eat anything but an inferior fish diet.

Strike Five: Heavy metals.

There is a great deal of persuasive research suggesting that predatory fish (those at the very top of the food chain and the same ones often found in pet food or used as 'treats' for cats) have extremely high levels of heavy metals such as mercury–in addition to pesticides and other toxins. A 2004 study published in Acta Neuropatholgica discovered neurological disturbances in young kittens fed daily with tuna containing the US FDA-approved level of mercury (0.5 ppm).

Strike Six: Possible link to hyperthyroidism.
A US Environmental Protection Agency (EPA) study in 2007 revealed a possible disturbing link between feline hyperthyroidism and the chemicals in fire retardants–that mimic thyroid hormones–and cats' consumption of canned food with fish. In the study, cats eating canned fish were exposed to polybrominated diphenyl ethers (PBDEs) at levels five times higher than cats eating poultry or beef canned foods. In 2016, a study in the American Chemical Society's Environmental Science and Technology suggested that fish-flavored cat foots could be among the culprits in escalating cases of hyperthyroidism in cats.

Strike Seven: Vitamin E depletion.
Felines love tuna, but eating it long term can deplete a cat's stores of vitamin E and create conditions that lead to an extraordinarily painful condition called steatitis, with symptoms such as hypersensitivity to touch and loss of appetite. Huuuuuge bummer for the cat and for you. You'll find tuna in lots of cat foods for the very reason that it's tasty to cats and draws them to the food. But it has nothing to do with healthy, safe, or necessary nutrition for cats.

Strike Eight? Allergenic.
Fish are allergenic. To my mind, it just makes little sense to feed something that is more likely to create a allergic reaction than something that isn't. Dr. Jean Hofve wisely advises against feeding fish and suggests that it be reserved as a very occasional and special treat–certainly no more than once a week.

If you're determined to give your cat a treat once in awhile, go for something like small bits of dehydrated chicken liver or freeze-dried chicken hearts. But skip the fish. If you must give treats, make it from something that had fur or feathers, not fins. It's safer for your carnivore.

CHAPTER EIGHTEEN

Anti-Parasite treatments/deworming and Flea Medications

"

I don't recommend routine deworming of dogs – ever. There isn't a universal dewormer that kills every parasite imaginable.

-Dr. Karen Becker

@drkarenbecker on X"

One of the Least Savory Aspects of Pet Ownership That You May Not Know About

This can be an invisible issue but it can cause symptoms in your dog or cat like vomiting, weight loss, diarrhea and poor coat condition. But it also may not cause any noticeable symptoms at all.

STORY AT-A-GLANCE

- Intestinal worms are relatively common in dogs and cats

- Four of the most common types are hookworms, roundworms, tapeworms and whipworms
- If you suspect your dog or cat is dealing with an intestinal worm infestation, prompt diagnosis and treatment will assure the best outcome
- Treatment should be targeted to the specific identified parasite; combination dewormers, especially those given monthly, should be avoided

There's a not-so-pleasant aspect of pet parenting that most of us are familiar with (and wish we weren't!) — the dreaded intestinal worm infestation. There are actually several types of worms that can wriggle their way into your dog's or cat's GI tract, including the hookworm, roundworm, tapeworm and whipworm.

Intestinal Parasites in Cats & Dogs

Intestinal parasites are worms and single-celled organisms (protozoa) that can exist in the digestive tract of dogs and cats. They can infect animals of any age, although puppies and kittens tend to be the most susceptible. Intestinal parasites vary in size and shape, and some are so small they must be diagnosed by antigen testing or microscopic evaluation. Others, like roundworms and tapeworms, can be visible in feces. Certain intestinal parasites are contagious to other animals and humans. Parasites attach themselves to the lining of the intestines. They suck blood and nutrients from food the animal has ingested. The result is damage to the intestinal lining and malabsorption of nutrients from food. Other parasites are passed to puppies or kittens through mother's placenta or milk. Infected animals may show no signs of infection, while others may suffer from diarrhea, weight loss, malnutrition, weakness, and blood loss. There are dozens of varied species and types of intestinal parasites, but only a few types that result in most of the parasitic infections in dogs and cats.

What are the most common intestinal parasites affecting dogs and cats?

Roundworms

Known as nematodes or ascarids, these are the most common intestinal parasites in dogs and cats. Adult roundworms are 3-5 inches long, cream-colored, and tubular shaped. Animals with roundworms pass the infection to other animals when the worm eggs develop into larvae and are present in the infected animal's feces. The larvae then inhabit the soil around the feces, leaving other animals (and children), vulnerable to accidental ingestion. In addition to diarrhea and weight loss, animals with roundworms can also exhibit a "potbellied" appearance, coughing, and the presence of worms passed in the feces. Diagnosis is made through the detection of roundworm eggs in feces using a microscope.

Roundworms are large and spaghetti-like in appearance, and they can create a full-blown infestation in your pet before you even know they're there. By the time you see signs of roundworms in your dog's or cat's feces or vomit, he's overrun with them.

It's important not to wait until you actually see the worms to alert you to an infestation. If you suspect your dog or cat has been exposed, you should collect a stool sample and drop it by your veterinarian's office for analysis.

Pets typically acquire roundworms by eating infected feces. The infection can also be passed from a female to her unborn litter across the placenta. The pups or kittens develop their own infection while still in the uterus and are born positive for roundworm.

Puppies and kittens with roundworm often have potbellies and poor growth. If not treated quickly, a severe infestation can block the intestines and cause death. That's why I recommend checking fecal samples at 6, 8, 10 and 12 weeks of age.

Hookworms

This is the second most common intestinal parasite found in dogs, but they are less common in cats. These are dangerous parasites in that they bite into the intestinal lining and suck blood. Pets also become infected when larvae penetrate the animal's skin or the lining of the mouth. Puppies are more vulnerable to infection than adult dogs; infected mothers pass larvae through their placenta, colostrum or milk. Severe cases can cause anemia and pneumonia. Diarrhea with dark, tarry feces signals internal bleeding and often accompanies severe infections. Diagnosis is made though identification of hookworm eggs in feces using a microscope.

Hookworms attach to the intestinal wall and suck the blood of the host. They're much more common in dogs than cats. Hookworms are primarily transmitted fecal-orally to animals, meaning your dog or cat may eat contaminated feces or dirt, or he might walk through contaminated soil, then lick his paws and ingest the eggs. Puppies and kittens can acquire hookworm from an infected mother's milk.

A puppy or kitten who acquires hookworms can become lethargic, weak, malnourished and anemic. It isn't uncommon for young pets to die from a hookworm infestation.

Infected adult pets may show symptoms of poor appetite and weight loss. Chronic hookworm infestation is a common cause of illness in older dogs.

Humans can also acquire a hookworm infection, typically by picking up the eggs or larvae on the skin from soil contaminated by infected wild animal or pet poop. Hookworm larvae have the ability to penetrate human skin, and they aren't visible to the naked eye.

To prevent a hookworm infestation, it's important to get rid of any potentially infective feces from wild or stray animals around your property that might tempt your dog or cat. It's also a good idea to keep your pet away from the poop of other animals while you're walking outdoors or hiking.

Whipworms

This parasite's name is inspired by their whip-like shape. They are more common in dogs than in cats. Adult whipworms are typically found in the colon and cecum (large intestine) of the animal. Eggs are passed in the feces and become infective in about 4 to 8 weeks. Once infective eggs are ingested, larvae develop in the small intestine and move to the colon where the adults mature. Whipworms bury their heads in the lining of the intestine and suck blood, but they are less harmful and do not cause health problems. Often, there are no clinical signs of light infections, but if not diagnosed and treated in a timely manner, an increase in the number of worms results in intestinal inflammation, followed by diarrhea, weight loss, and blood loss. Whipworm eggs remain viable in soil for years.

Whipworms are more common in dogs than cats, and pets can only be infected by ingesting whipworm eggs from soil or other substrates containing eggs. In the small intestine, larvae hatch from ingested eggs and burrow into the mucosal lining. From two to 10 days later, they move on to the cecum and grow into adult worms.

The eggs are not infectious when passed in feces. They need several weeks in soil to develop into infective larvae inside their shells. A dog or cat eats contaminated soil or objects in the soil and the cycle of infection begins.

Adult whipworms look like tiny pieces of thread, with one end enlarged. They are rarely seen in in feces. Many pets show no signs of illness with a whipworm infestation. Symptoms when they do occur can include bloody diarrhea, dehydration, weight loss, anemia and even death in severe cases.

Re-infection with whipworm from contaminated environments is a significant concern. The eggs are extremely resilient and resistant to most cleaning methods and even freezing temperatures. They can be dried out with strong agents like agricultural lime, but the preferred method is to replace contaminated soil with new soil or another substrate.

Regularly picking up poop from your yard and other areas your pet frequents will help reduce the risk of further contamination of soil.

Tapeworms

Also known as cestodes, tapeworms are segmented worms that get their name from their thin and flat appearance. Dogs and cats become infected when they eat infected fleas or lice. Animals that have access to small mammals (i.e., rodents) infected with these worms are also at risk. It is important to note that since tapeworm eggs do not show up well in routine fecal analyses, your veterinarian should be notified if you see rice-like segments near your pet's tail. In addition to common symptoms associated with parasitic infection, a shaggy coat, and colic may be present. There may be no signs in mild cases.

Tapeworms are flat-shaped, with a head, neck and many body segments called proglottids. The head has suckers and hooks that allow the tapeworm to deeply embed into the walls of the small intestine. The worms can range from under an inch to several feet (yes, feet!) in length.

Tapeworm segments are often seen near the anus of an infected pet, and segments that have been recently passed out of the body may still be moving.

Your dog or cat can acquire a tapeworm infestation by eating part or all of an intermediate host (e.g., birds, fish, reptiles and rats) carrying tapeworm eggs, larvae or cysts. Fleas and lice also harbor tapeworm eggs.

The most common method of transmission is through ingestion of adult fleas, birds, rodents, rabbits or through scavenging.

Free-roaming pets with access to freshly killed wild or domestic animals are at increased risk of acquiring tapeworms, as are animals with heavy lice and/or flea infestations.

Pets with tapeworms often show no signs of discomfort. When symptoms do occur, they can include itchiness around the anus, licking of the anal and perianal area, butt scooting, weight loss without loss of appetite, increased appetite without weight gain, poor coat or skin condition, distended or painful abdomen, diarrhea, lethargy and irritability.

Rarely, a heavy infestation of adult tapeworms causes partial or complete intestinal blockage, which is a true medical emergency. These parasites can be difficult to diagnose, and sometimes the only noticeable symptom is what looks like grains of white rice (tapeworm segments) stuck to or crawling through the fur around a pet's rear end.

Coccidia

These are single-celled parasites (protozoa) that are not visible to the naked eye. Like many intestinal parasites, coccidia are very contagious among puppies and kittens as their immune systems might not yet be strong enough to fight off the infection. Dogs will show signs of infection more often than cats. Treatment may be unnecessary in cats because they usually eliminate the infection themselves. Pets become infected by eating infected soil or licking contaminated paws or fur. Bloody, watery diarrhea may be present, with the potential for dehydration. The presence of coccidia is detected through a routine fecal test.

Giardia

Like coccidia, giardia is a single-celled protozoan that attaches and multiplies in the small intestine, damaging the intestinal lining and reducing the absorption of nutrients from food. They produce cysts that pass through the feces. The cysts survive well in the environment and only a small number of organisms are needed to cause infection. As a result, Giardia is harder to diagnose than other intestinal parasites, and several stool samples may have to be tested before it is found. Giardia infection sometimes shows no clinical signs in dogs or cats. In more severe cases, it can cause weight loss and diarrhea, abnormal feces (soft, pale and foul-smelling), and vomiting.

Giardia By Dr. Karen Becker

Giardia are flagellated protozoa, or one-celled organisms that live not only in the small intestine of dogs and cats, but also in most wild animals and, actually, in a lot of people living in third-world countries. There's much that isn't known about the giardia parasite. We don't know how many species there are exactly and which ones affect which animals. We also don't know everything about the life cycle of all the giardia species. It's generally assumed that while infection with giardia is common, acquiring disease from the infection is less common.

Giardia is ubiquitous in the environment. It's all over. It's out there in rivers, ponds, and puddles. It can be found in a whole bunch of places. It's also zoonotic, meaning that if the family dog has it or the family member has it, the entire rest of the family – humans and animals – can be infected with it. Puppies acquired from puppy mills and other facilities that house lots of dogs commonly carry the giardia parasite.

Causes of Giardia Infection in Pets

A dog gets giardia by ingesting an infected cyst shed by another animal's poop or in another animal's feces. Contamination can occur directly or indirectly with contact of these infected cysts. The most common route of a transmission is through contaminated water. The giardia parasite prefers cool, moist environments. Once inside a dog or cat's small intestine, the cyst opens and releases the active form of the parasite. These forms are then able to move around and attach themselves to the walls of the intestine, where they reproduce via dividing in two. They split into two. Eventually, giardia encysts (builds a cyst around itself) and they're passed out from a dog or cat's body in the feces. Those feces can contaminate the soil, grass, water, or wherever dogs or cats poop. This also means that if your dog is giardia-positive and licks her butt, then licks another pack member, then there's a potential for transmission to occur this way.

Signs and Symptoms

The majority of giardia infections are asymptomatic, meaning there's no obvious symptoms that your dog is infected. When symptoms are present, the most common one is diarrhea, which can be acute, chronic, or fluctuant. Many dog owners don't consult their veterinarians about their dog's soft, mushy stools, because oftentimes the stool improves on its own. About the time that you're considering calling your veterinarian – about loose stool – oftentimes, the stool firms up and all seems to be well. The owner just assumes that maybe the dog got into something or ate something that didn't agree with him. The cases of giardia then continue to go undiagnosed. After a week, a month, or sometimes years of undiagnosed giardia infection, a giardia positive animal can experience an acute and very debilitating bout of bloody, dehydrating diarrhea. Most dogs with diarrhea will not lose their appetite, but they often times – with chronic cases – lose a lot of body weight.

A giardia infection interferes with digestion and inhibits absorption of nutrients. It can also damage the lining of the intestine. In fact, this particular parasite is one reason why we can see chronic GI inflammation in dogs and cats. I get a lot of referrals at my hospital for inflammatory bowel disease. Many of my IBD patients have a history of being giardia-positive when they were little kitties or little puppies. I also see a number of pets with chronic diarrhea that suffer from malabsorption and other digestive issues, who actually end up being giardia-positive.

Giardia Diagnosis in Pets

Diagnosis of giardia is done through a special fecal test. If you're trying to determine on your own by looking at your dog or cat's poop to see if your dog or cat is giardiapositive, don't bother, because this particular parasite is microscopic. You won't see any evidence by examining your pet's poop. In 2009, I read an article suggesting that in-house parasite analysis testing – which means stool tests that are checked in your vet's clinic – were yielding up to 30 percent false-negative results. This means that vets were erroneously telling clients that their pets were parasite-free, when they actually weren't. I decided to test this theory and sent all of my fecal samples to our local laboratory versus in-house testing for a more comprehensive stool analysis. Interestingly, the number of giardia-positive pets in my practice began to increase. I believe that national veterinary labs like Antech and Idexx, which use standardized equipment that returns consistent reliable results, reduce the amount of fecal in-house testing errors. There are also some parasites like giardia, which may not consistently be shed in every pet's stool sample. This is why I recommend any patient with a history of bowel problems be tested for giardia with an ELISA test. A fecal ELISA test is different than a fecal flotation examination. Because not every giardia-positive patient sheds a cyst in every stool sample, an ELISA test checks for giardia antigens present in the animal's body versus looking for actual cysts in the stool. Many vets don't routinely run this test. If your pet is suffering from chronic diarrhea, make sure you ask for a fecal antigen test in addition to a regular fecal float.

Unfortunately, giardia is growing resistant to many of the common antiprotozoal medications – with a result being that pets can become persistent carriers. If your pet has been tested positive for giardia, hopefully your dog or cat has cleared the infection successfully after treatment. Because the ELISA test can show positive for up to six months after treatment as all the giardia antigens are being cleared out of your pet's system, it's important that you check your pet several times. We recommend once a month for three to four months with a fecal float afterwards to make sure that he or she is really negative. As I mentioned, dogs don't shed the cyst in every stool sample, so checking multiple times is a really good idea. This might seem confusing, but the diagnostic test for giardia – the ELISA test – isn't a good post-treatment follow-up test. If that makes any sense – hopefully, it does.

Protect Your Pets from Giardia Infection

How to avoid giardia? Avoid kenneling your pets with a bunch of other animals, pick up your own animal's feces outside, and avoid walking your dog where other animals have pooped. To the best of your ability, I recommend not letting your dog drink from puddles of water that are outside. Any source of outdoor contaminated water is a potential source for giardia. Most importantly, check a fecal sample through your vet's diagnostic lab twice a year to identify and remove parasites before they can cause a tremendous amount of GI inflammation. On one side note, I don't recommend routine deworming for dogs ever. There isn't one universal dewormer that kills all parasites, meaning that there isn't one dewormer that would get rid of giardia, coccidia, and tapeworm with all one pill. I don't recommend assuming that your pet has these parasites and offering unnecessary medications. I also don't recommend using natural dewormers periodically to get rid of parasites that your pet may not even have. I have seen all too often at my practice many cases of really significant GI inflammation from unnecessary doses of strong herbal preparations that are totally unnecessary, because the dog doesn't have parasites in the first place. I do recommend routinely and proactively testing your dog's or cat's poop to make sure that the pet is truly parasite-negative, versus giving any medication that simply isn't necessary.

How are parasite infections treated?

Conventional treatment uses deworming medication. Medications like pyrantel can produce side effects including nausea, vomiting, lack of appetite and diarrhea. Side effects of other common medications include dizziness, cough, dark urine, and black tarry stools. These side effects mimic the symptoms of the infection themselves, making it difficult to differentiate between a symptom of the infection and a medication side effect. Do your research on the chemicals used in recommended products including dosage and instructions for use, as well as side effects.

There are safe and natural remedies for deworming your pet. They can be used to treat an active infection as well as prevent one.

Fruits & Vegetables

Fruits and veggies that are high in fiber (carrots, banana, apple, coconut, and papaya) act as natural de-wormers. Grate them into your pet's bowl. Dosage is 1 tsp per 10 pounds body weight. Fermented vegetables are a great natural de-wormer—in addition to boosting the immune system, they can also help expel the parasites. Pomegranate is useful for eliminating tapeworms.

Seeds

Pumpkin seeds contain an amino acid called Cucurbitin that paralyzes the worms and eliminates them from the digestive tract. Serve ¼ tsp per 10 pounds of ground seed once or twice daily until the parasites are gone. Black cumin seeds (whole) are safe and effective for most worms. Use ½-1 tsp daily in food. Heat the seeds in a pan to get rid of the bitter taste.

Garlic

For use in dogs in moderate amounts: dosage is ¼ clove per 10 pounds body weight daily. Chop the garlic and let it sit for 10-15 minutes before adding it to your pet's food. Do not use garlic to fight worms in pregnant or lactating dogs.

Apple Cider Vinegar

Can be used in both dogs and cats. It creates a more alkaline digestive system that's less attractive to parasites. Use raw organic, unfiltered ACV and give ¼-1 tsp in your pet's water or food.

Herbs?

Herbs like thyme and parsley are natural de-wormers. Thyme is especially useful for hookworms. Add one tsp per pound of food. Cook fresh parsley down, strain out the solids, and freeze them into ice cubes. Give one cube daily.

Natural Pet De-wormer Products

Homeopathic remedies, essential oils, and other natural pet de-wormer products can be powerful additions to your pet's regimen. Be sure to purchase from a reputable company and read the reviews of the product before purchase.

Food Grade Diatomaceous Earth (DE)

Add in ¼ tsp for small dogs up to 1 tsp for dogs over 55 pounds. DE actually rids the body of roundworms, whipworms, pinworms, and hookworms within 7 days of being fed daily. But to be most effective, it must be fed long enough to catch all newly hatching eggs or cycling of the worms through the lungs and back to the stomach as DE does not kill the eggs.

Can parasitic infestations be prevented?

The short answer is YES! A pet's strong immune system can keep parasite infections under control. Parasites tend to proliferate in weak, sick, stressed, malnourished, overvaccinated and neglected animals. A species-appropriate diet is the best line of defense to prevent parasitic infections. Keep your pet's immune system strong by adding mushroom powders, tinctures, antioxidants and probiotics to their daily nutrition regimen.

Sanitation is important, especially in kennels or catteries where large numbers of animals are housed. Feces should be removed and disposed of frequently, and fecal contamination of feed and water should be prevented. Runs, cages, and utensils should be disinfected daily. Insect control is also important. Pet parents should employ their own good hygiene and wash hands after handling their animals.

Be sure your veterinarian includes annual fecal testing as part of your pet's annual examination. Fecal samples should be checked more frequently if your dog or cat prefers to spend most of its time outdoors. A fecal test on a fresh sample should be performed following treatment of an infection to make sure all parasites have been cleared.

Even though in most cases, intestinal parasitic infestation is not a life-threatening situation, it can lead to various clinical problems. If left untreated, it can become a public health issue. Deworming is an important preventative care regime for reducing parasites and improving your pet's health. Fruits, vegetables, seeds, herbs and homeopathic extracts are all great natural alternatives to prescribed deworming medications. Keep your pet's immune system at optimal health, and parasites won't find a welcoming environment!

How Do I Know If My Pet Has Worms?

The short answer: it can be challenging. Some intestinal worms can be seen with the naked eye; others can't. Dogs and cats with worm infestations may have one or more of the following symptoms:

1. Diarrhea that may or may not be bloody
2. Vomiting
3. Weight loss
4. Poor coat condition

However, sometimes the presence of intestinal worms causes no noticeable symptoms. The worms can also lay dormant in your pet's body for long stretches. The following is a short primer on four common types of intestinal worms.

Choose Targeted Treatment and Avoid Combination Dewormers

As with any illness in your dog or cat, the earlier an intestinal worm infestation is diagnosed and treated, the better the outcome. Many veterinarians include a stool check as part of the wellness exam. If yours doesn't, you can request it. It's important to note that tapeworms can be difficult to diagnose with routine stool sample tests, so be sure to keep an eye out for the appearance of "rice" either in your pet's poop or in the fur around his rear end.

It's very important that your veterinarian identifies the precise type of worm that has invaded your pet's intestinal tract. I recommend avoiding combination treatments that claim to kill and/or prevent a variety of worms and other internal parasites. They are typically prescribed for monthly use.

More is not better when it comes to drugs for your pet. If your dog or cat has whipworms, for example, treat the whipworms specifically, and only long enough to clear the infection. Some integrative veterinarians offer natural dewormers for certain kinds of intestinal worm infestations. I have tried them all and unfortunately, sometimes they work, and sometimes they don't.

For instance, food-grade diatomaceous earth kills tapeworm segments, but not the deeply embedded head, so you may think you've killed the entire worm, only to find out later that your pet is chronically infected, which can lead to chronic GI inflammation and dysbiosis.

It's fine to try natural deworming first, but making sure these resilient parasites are truly eliminated, regardless of what you use, is of utmost importance to avoid chronic, avoidable GI problems.

FLEAS

If you are sitting on the edge of your seat for this one, sit back and relax, as there are no easy answers to the flea problern. The most important measure vou can take is similar to that with any illness, and that is to strengthen the overall health of the animal. In general, given the same environment, healthier animals suffer less from fleas. It all comes back to good food, lots of love, and minimal stress. Cleanliness is important also, but healthy cats generally stay clean.

Success against flea infestations depends heavily upon control of the flea life cycle off of the animal. The life cycle is similar to that of the butterfly with egg, larva, cocoon, and adult stages. The following is the life cycle for *Ctenocephalides felis*, the "cat flea." This flea accounts for 99 percent of fleas on cats and 85 - 95 percent of fleas on dogs. *Pulex irritans*, the "human flea," is next in frequently on dogs, and the "dog flea," *Ctenocephalides canis*, is last, although possibly more common in the northeast United States.

Although fleas live on the skin of our cats and dogs, they lay eggs that fall off and hatch in the environment rather than on the animal. These eggs hatch into small (one-fourth inch long), wormlike larvae after two to five days at 70 to 80 percent humidity. If the humidity is less than 30 to 40 percent, the eggs will not hatch. Larvae are clear to white with a reddish-brown streak of blood pigment in their intestines; you may see the larvae where your companion sleeps. The larvae must eat adult flea feces to develop further.

Larvae are very susceptible to heat and drying; they will die if the relative humidity drops below 50 percent. Continued temperatures above 95 F (35 C) will also kill the larvae. For these and other reasons, the larvae shy away from light and tend to travel downward. Thus, they develop at the base of carpet pile or grasses, under furniture, and under porches.

After one to two weeks, the larva spins a cocoon, where development continues as it transforms into a "pre-emerged adult. It takes one to three weeks to make this transition, but these pre-emerged adults do not issue from the cocoon until an external stimulus triggers them to hatch. They may sit patiently in the cocoon for up to 140 days, waiting for a host to arrive. While in the cocoon, the flea is protected from insecticides and other external threats. Once the correct stimulus occurs, the flea can break out of the cocoon and leap onto the host in less than a second. They are virtually not exposed, even to residual insecticides.

What stimuli entices these pre-emerged adults to emerge? Heat is the primarv agent, but vibration, moisture, physical pressure, and carbon dioxide will also incite hatching—essentially, anything that tells the flea that a warm-blooded animal is available. A vacuum cleaner with a beater bar can sometimes trick the flea into emerging, thus we can use this to our advantage.

Adult fleas must live on the animal, though they can survive for one to two weeks before finding a host. Once they feed, however, they can only survive for up to four days, and most will die after two days. The adult life span may exceed one hundred days. Eggs are laid on the animal and drop onto the floor or ground, so the highest concentration of eggs, larvae , and cocoons will be where the animal spends the majority of its time.

The female flea must feed constantly to lay eggs, as she may lay up to twice her body weight daily in eggs. This amounts to as many as forty-six eggs per day in the first week of life, and over two thousand eggs over a one-hundred-day life span. In order to accomplish this feat she will consume fifteen times her weight in blood every day. Although this may not sound like a lot of blood relative to the host, with large numbers of fleas on puppies and kittens the impact can be severe, even fatal.

Although freezing temperatures can kill fleas in the winter, they survive in houses and in protected spaces like piles of leaves and yard waste, and in crawl spaces under houses. Additionally, other host species such as raccoons and opossums may host these fleas. Squirrels do not host this species of flea, however.

How, then, can we control this adaptable parasite? Diligence rather than toxic chemicals is our best ally. Strong chemicals only weaken your companion's health in the long run, making her more susceptible to fleas and other diseases. We now know that these chemicals can also affect us, even if they are applied to our companion animals, so the gain is not worth the risk in my opinion.

These chemicals also kill other life forms and end up in our drinking water, foods, and Mother's milk. DDT is still ubiquitous, even though its usage in the United States was stopped years ago.

Flea control has two main realms. First is reducing the adult fleas on the animal, including reducing egg production. Second is to reduce the stages that live in the environment, off the animal. This includes the house and the yard.

For control of adult fleas on your companion, use nontoxic materials. Shampoos can drastically reduce adult fleas and will interfere with egg laying even if the fleas are not all killed. You usually do not need to use a chemical flea shampoo, most shampoos kill fleas if you lather well and wait ten to fifteen minutes before rinsing(drown them on your pet's body). Be sure to rinse well to avoid irritating and drying the skin.

Herbal rinses can repel fleas; lavender, eucalyptus, and pennyroyal work fairly well for dogs. I would not use the latter two on cats as they can be toxic to cats. You can use a lemon rinse: steep a cut-up lemon or two in a quart of boiling water and allow to cool. Use the liquid as a rinse or sponge it onto the coat. Skin-so-Soft bv Avon is a bath oil that repels fleas. Use one to one and one-half ounces per gallon of water and apply as a rinse or spray. It is somewhat oily, thus it is better on outside animals and on animals with coarse coats.

Black walnut leaves and cedar shavings can be used in bedding to repel fleas. Flea combs are fine-toothed combs that will mechanically remove fleas. They also disrupt feeding and egg laying. These work well on short haired animals. You can comb first with a wide-toothed comb to make it easier for the flea comb to get through the coat.

Once you catch the fleas on the comb, drop them into soapv water (otherwise they sit on the surface and can jump out of the container) and flush this down the toilet. You can also use alcohol to collect the fleas.

Diatomaceous earth is somewhat effective on the animal as well as in the house. It mechanically damages the flea's intestines and respiratory apparatus, killing the flea. The only safety concern for you or your animals is breathing the dust, so don't make a cloud when you apply the powder. Supplements such as brewer's yeast and garlic help 20 to 25 percent of animals repel fleas, though some animals are allergic to yeast and may develop diarrhea or skin problems.

I do not recommend the following types of agents: Ultrasonic collars do not work and they are audible (ninety decibels at forty kilohertz—very loud) to cats and dogs. Hearing disturbance and behavior modification has been documented. Topical or oral products for flea control may work rather well in some cases, but it is illogical to assume they are safe. Anything that can kill one species cannot be completely safe for another species. I have heard and seen problems with any of these programs, including reactions that threatened death. I don't believe these spot treatments give our companions an advantage. D-limonene (a citrus derivative) is said to be safe for dogs but I know of several poisonings, especially in cats, and I do not recommend this product. Flea collars work poorly and are very toxic to animals and everyone they live around. Dips and other chemicals are simply too unsafe for the pet, you and the planet.

For household control, diligent cleanliness is the most

important part of the equation. Concentrate under furniture and where vour companions spend the majority of their time. Vacuumn daily at first, then taper to weekly. Shampoos and steam cleaners add moisture to carpets and thus mav initiate hatching of fleas. This can be good if you follow closely thorough vacuuming.

If you need to apply a flea-killing agent, boron cornpounds are fairlv effective and very safe. Wondercide & Fleabusters are two companies that use E.O as one of these compounds. Twenty Mule Borax is a laundry additive that is also effective and is inexpensive, though it requires application every few months. You can buy it in most grocerv stores. Sprinkle it on carpets or floors and use a broom to work it into the carpet pile or into cracks between wood or tiles. Allow it to stay overnight and then vacuum. Repeat two weeks after the first application, then every few months, as needed. Although this is very safe (I know of no instances of poisoning), it is wise to keep animals out of the room while applying the product, and try not to stir up a cloud of dust to breathe. You could also wear a gas mask during application. For smooth floors, mopping with a solution of about a cup of borax per gallon of water works as well, though it leaves a slightly dull appearance. You can follow in few days with a sponge mop to regain the shine if desired. Maximum effectiveness is reached about two weeks after application, so be patient if you still see fleas after a few clays.

Diatomaceous earth is also somewhat effective in the house and is applied in essentially the same manner. Some people mix the borax and diatomaceous earth together for application. As a last resort, you can use a natural pyrethrin such as a powder of pyrethrum flowers to get a quick handle on the household infestation if it is severe. Even this is toxic, though it breaks clown rather quickly.Finally, outside control is difficult, but there are some rmeasures that help. Keep the yard cut short and clippings raked to minimize protected areas (remember that heat and low hunli(liry as well as freezing will kill fleas). Treat dog houses or areas where anirnals sleep with diatonraceous earth, and use cedar shavings or black walnut leaves. There is a nematode (worm) that parasitizes fleas and kills them; this can be applied during flea season (warm, humid weather) to reduce the flea burden in the yard. Many garden and hardware stores sell these nematodes. They are also available through the catalog "Gardens Alive," which specializes in nontoxic gardening.

There is little that homeopathy has to offer flor flea control other than constitutional treatment to improve health and resistance to fleas. Pulex irritans is a remedy made from the human flea, and some feel that it can improve resistance.

Sulphur is the remedy most often associated with flea infestation, though it is by no means the only remedv for this. I have even heard it suggested that a spray made of 30C Sulphur in water will repel fleas. I have not tried this, however, and I am not sure of its wisdom, as the animal and the guardian are dosed with the remedy at each application. *Ledum palustre* is the big remedy for insect bites and puncture wounds and thus is recommended bv some for the reaction to the flea bite. *Caladium* is a remedy for insect bites that sting and burn excessively It may help some animals who are especially sensitive to flea bites.

Allergies are not caused by the allergen- -they are an

internal problem first. The immune system becomes overreactive and then develops an allergy to whatever potential allergens are around. A flea allergy is not caused by fleas; rather the dog is already potentially allergic and fleas are cornrnon, so he develops an allergy to the flea saliva. The immune system must be compromised first, and this is often caused by other stressors like vaccines, toxins, and poor foods.Once the allergy is present, however, the continued allergic reaction may keep the dog from responding to treatment, so the allergens must be avoided as much as possible until the sensitivity can be diminished. If fleas are the problem, flea control is essential; if food allergies are present, those foods must be avoided until the allergy lessens through treatment.

CHAPTER NINETEEN

The Vaccination Question

Introduction

Prevention is powerful. It provides us with something intangible and yet priceless - peace of mind. What are we willing to do to obtain it? It turns out, quite a bit, which makes us exploitable. We have been sold a bill of goods about the safety and effectiveness of vaccines and dewormers/anti-parasitics and the lack of other alternatives. The conventional medical cartel has stepped over its opposition and its victims alike, seeking profit and control, and not allowing true science to impede it in any way, the truth still found its way. It will continue to find its way to those who have eyes to see and ears to hear.

It's time for us to take back the responsibility we've carelessly given away. We don't want to blame ourselves if our pet dies from an infection, so we leave it to the vet. We don't want to deal with our pet's diet, so we trust pet food companies. We don't want to take care of our own health, so we hand it over to big tech and the medical industry. As someone who used to follow the crowd, I can tell you that the dangers of vaccines are becoming more known. Sadly, most people think they have no other choice and think that the risk is worth it, for the peace of mind they desperately seek. But that's not true at all.

Since life began on this planet, pathogens and their hosts have danced together in a delicate balance. The first meeting between them is usually rocky, resulting in many deaths within the host species. Perhaps the same is true for the parasite species. But how would we know? Since we are not counting their deaths.

All species have one thing in common, the survival instinct. Every single living thing on this planet desires to live: from a giant whale to the tiniest microbe. And what does any parasitic species need to fulfill that desire? It needs a host and a live one at that. So is killing a host counterproductive to that need? You bet it is. The host also wants to survive, so not having immunity against a parasite microbe is counterproductive. After the first tragic meeting, both the host and the parasite realize that they must change if they want to fulfill their life function. We always think of a host species acquiring immunity against a killer microbe. But the other side of it is that the microbe will also mutate into a less virulent form in order not to kill its host. You see, the parasite never means to kill the host because without the host, what would happen to the parasite?

Nature is a bit crude in the way it achieves balance, but it always gets the job done. And it could continue to get the job done, even without human intervention. When a species is faced with the prospect of annihilation from an encounter with a new disease, if left alone, it will naturally acquire immunity, which will then be passed on to future generations. At the same time, that particular disease will mellow its form to stop killing the host. So why is it in our human nature to interfere?

It is because we are individual beings concerned with individual life. Animals, on the other hand, are concerned with the survival of their species. Most of what animals do is about saving the species and most of what humans do is about saving the individual. A whelping bitch will not stop to retrieve one last puppy until all of them are born. A single penguin will march to his death when he falls behind the flock, but will not turn around and head back towards the ocean where he would have survived. These are examples of the instinct to preserve the species, of the oversoul of the species guiding each individual animal, as opposed to looking for self-interest or acting out of an emotion as people do. It is not good or bad. It just is. Please do not compare this concept with the idea of collectivism and 'the greater good', special interest groups promote for their own agenda; experimenting on lab animals for the greater good does not improve any species, especially human. Being human means being ethical and animal experiments are anything but ethical.

So why am I telling you all this? So that you can see more clearly where this desire to immunize and deworm comes from. Let us look at the time when the parvo virus broke out and a lot of puppies died, a reasoning mind would have concluded that this was a temporary situation, which it was, and that within the next generation or two, immunity would have been achieved without our interference, but we humans are emotional creatures. None of us wanted puppies to die when riding the overwhelming wave of sadness and fear. We don't care about the species. We just want to save our puppy. Am I right?

It is precisely this play on our emotions that opened the door for pharmaceutical companies to sell us on the idea of vaccinations, dewormers and anti-flea/tick drugs. A fearful mind is not a reasoning mind. The more we are afraid of the pathogens, the more vaccines, deworming medications and flea topicals they get to sell. The more diseases emerge because of these intervening practices, the more drugs they get to sell. You see the minds in charge of the pharmaceutical industry are not emotional. They are rather very calculative. Is the mortality rate really impacted by these practices? Let's explore.

One thing is for sure, nature loves balance, life and death are part of that balance. If you try to get rid of the disease, that is all you get (just look at all the chronically sick animals in the world whose disease cause by malnutrition is exasberated by the combination of vaccinations, deworming & flea medications.). If you try to get rid of death, death is all you get - It is the law of attraction at work. While they are preventing puppies from dying of infectious diseases, which are meant to cleanse the species, more and more dogs are being euthanized due to behavioral problems such as aggression and chronic health issues. Many behavioral problems are a direct consequence of vaccination(such as aggression in animals never known to be aggressive before) because every vaccine causes a disease and affects the entire organism including the mind. The rabies vaccine is notorious for inducing aggression, something I have witnessed firsthand.

Nature being a crude balance achiever keeps the rate of death constant. You don't want to give up young pups?

She'll take the adults. You don't want them to die of infectious disease? When they go 'nuts' or become disabled, you will take them out yourself.

Picture the situation and see if it seems as senseless to you as it does to me. Animal Shelters, vaccinate and deworm all dogs and puppies. I have seen it firsthand as well as a die-off that occurs about a week later among the pups. Unfortunately, ignorance will stop these well-meaning people from examining the facts. They are well-intentioned efforts, aimed at protecting the pups from diseases and saving their lives. Right? Because most people want to adopt a healthy puppy, they will simply simultaneously put down adult dogs that nobody wants, as well as those that have behavioral problems or bad hips.

You want to bet that the death rate stays the same? Here is an opportunity to let nature pick and nature will always let the most stable survive, an opportunity to let the dog species work on its own immunity and improve itself amidst the dire conditions and an opportunity for dogs to rise like the phoenix from the ashes of tragedy, neglect and abandonment and become stronger with each generation. But that opportunity is not taken. It wouldn't be politically correct. Injecting their little bodies with cocktails of poisons apparently is.

Imagine what would happen if homeopathic remedies were used for immunization as well as treatment within animal shelters. The animals would be healthier and more mentally stable, which would result in a lower return rate. The cost of care would plummet - the right solution, everyone wins.

Ethical action means doing no harm. I'm not advocating letting the dog suffer and just standing by and watching, although as far as a species go, it would be better than vaccination. Through medicine proper we can do both : prevent a disease and cure it if it's already developed. A healthy cat fed a species appropriate diet is less suspectible to pathogens, parasites and infections. A cat that gets sick and then recovers imprints the future generations with the information on how to fight against that particular disease. Immunization, cure and healing are ethical and beneficial to the species. Vaccination is not.

What impact does vaccination have on the species? By vaccinating every individual animal and not allowing it to develop its own immunity we're effectively preventing the passing of the immunity to the future generations. A vaccine is always made from the most virulent form of the virus. Since pharmaceutical companies jump on the wagon, as soon as a disease appears and the level of fear is at its highest. While in nature, this virus would have mutated into a less virulent form. It does not so in the vaccine, generations of animals are therefore injected with the worst form of the virus and stripped off their natural immune response which would have been passed on to subsequent generations.

What is passed forward instead is deformed DNA and the destruction of the species must ensue. Vaccinated mothers do not pass on herd immunity, which then puts pup in greater danger of contracting disease while they are very young. By attempting to save the individual animal, we are effectively destroying the species. A healthy species is able to survive without human interference and we are taking this ability away from our animals. Since vaccines are known to cause even the acute form of the disease they are meant to prevent, many times dogs suffer double destruction: that of the individual which weakens or dies due to the vaccine and that of the species which is not allowed to evolve its immunity.

Who of you is willing to stand aside and watch your puppy die if need be in order to save the species of a dog? The good news is you don't have to. There is a way to protect the individual and actually improve the species as well. When ethical action is performed everyone benefits such as a case with homeopathic immunization or prophylaxis.

Disease is dynamic in nature and is first it is first experienced on the etheric level. If the lesson a disease is offering becomes resolved on the etheric level, there is no need to experience it on the physical level. The ultimate spiritual purpose behind every disease is to improve the species and the individual. There is a reason for everything, therefore, also for the disease. By administrating homeopathic prophylaxis we offer the experience and the lesson of the disease on the etheric level, and no physical suffering is needed. It is like pressing a fast forward button on evolution. Moving through the experience without having to suffer is an improvement over nature. Nature's way is crude, it accomplishes the goal, but through suffering and some losses Homeopathic prophylaxis allows the individual to experience disease in a very different refined fashion, with all the benefits, benefits and without the losses. Interested?

For more details on Homeopathic Nososdes and how to

administer them, see Alexandra Mikic's excellent free Kindle book 'Immune Doggy'.

The Secret Life of Microbes

In the history of microbiology, there seems to be a missing chapter - the part about *pleomorphic*(from Greek meaning many forms) nature of microbes. It's true that really they really are the shapeshifters.

The entire conventional medicine system is based on the assumption that the organism is basically aseptic does not contain microbes, and that the presence of microbes always means external invasion. This premise was brought forward by Louis Pasteur, and he is the only one medical books discuss, but Louis Pasteur had a contemporary Antoine Bechamp who maintained the pleomorphic theory of microbes. Bechamp allowed for certain infections being an external affairs, but he also understood that the microbes readily change their form in response to the internal environment of the organism.

Conventional science is based on the following outdated dogmas:

1. The smallest living unit is a cell.

2. The human body is aseptic and all microbes that are present must have entered from the outside.

3. Microbes are monomorphic(they have unique stable form, which is not changeable).

Pleumorphic theory states a:

1. A cell is not a primary living unit. There are trying tiny primordial biological units actually living inside the cells.

2. The organism is not sterile, but inhabited with many micro organisms which coexist in homeostasis when the terrain is healthy.

3. Micro organisms change their form and go through a definittive growth cycle in response to the change in

internal terrain.

Antoine Bechamp as well as many researchers after him couldn't deny the evidence they saw after carefully observing microorganisms. Bacterial forms readily arise out of the primordial living units in response to the presence of some dead tissue. They act as scavengers, the vultures of the body keeping it clean and removing debris. The forms became more virulent the further away from homeostasis the organism moved. Bacterial forms would metamorphose into fungal and viral forms.

Being colonized by micro organisms is natural and necessary for many life processes. But a disturbance in the internal milieu causes them to evolve into increasingly pathogenic forms. The proof of the pleomorphic theory was not the original goal for the scientists, simply a natural conclusion of their observations.

All scientists who came after Bechamp and Pasteur(among them Rife, Gerson, Naessens, Enderlain and Chachoua) were schooled in Pasteur's theory and struggled with themselves in the face of indisputable evidence to the contrary. Due to the suppression of the pleomorphic theory and its exclusion from the scientific curriculum, each of these scientists were quite literally on their own and starting from scratch. They had, however, all arrived at the same conclusion without knowing about each other's research or about Antoine Bechamp.

Gerson struggled to accept the undeniable truth of the importance of internal terrain as he saw how the cancers that arose out of the poisoned organisms would regress under the full oxidation of the system. He devised potassium based diets and saw health return to many.

Rife came upon the pleomorphic nature of the microorganisms when he noticed a change in the cancer culture he left standing. He isolated four different forms of the cancer microbe and also showed that they are changeable and can revert to the least pathogenic form, which he named bx. Rife was able to kill the pathogenic form of the microbe by targeting it the specific frequency ray. Many other pathogenic forms of different diseases succumbed to the rays of their specific frequencies, but you won't read about it in medical journals.

Before Rife, German microbiologist Enderlein proved that pathogenic microorganisms develop within the body and certain conditions exist, namely a change in acid-alkaline balance, lack of certain minerals and poor nutrition. Hyperacidity causes non pathogenic forms of micro organisms to evolve towards their virulent forms. Enderlein's research showed that primitive forms live in strong alkaline pH and bacterial forms live in a mild alkaline pH, fungal forms in a medium acid pH and viral forms live in strong acid pH.

Naessens' research concentrated on the primal living units within the cells which he named Somatids. He discovered that these units are indestructible, and at the same time, have 16 stages of development. The first three stages are highly beneficial, with the remaining stages being increasingly toxic. The change was triggered by the weakening of the immune system, due to traumas of different origins, which always meant a change in the internal environment.

Chachoua was focused on the resistance of animal organisms to the disease and also the resistance of certain organs within the organism, particularly the small intestine. He became interested in spontaneous remission from cancer that was preceded by a severe infection. This led to the lead to his nemesis theory, and then to tagging the cancer cells to make them more visible to the immune system. He kept noticing new micro organisms appearing in his cultures that could only be explained by pleomorphism.

Different scientists, different paths and different aims, but the same conclusion: microorganisms are pleomorphic. Pleomorphism is two directional meaning that microorganisms shift towards pathogenic forms triggered by the disturbance within the internal milieu, and they also revert to the non pathogenic forms and the balance is established once again.

Another thing that all scientists had in common was persecution by the official medical establishment -heavy fines, exclusion from the media, sealed laboratories, confiscated equipment, destroyed documentation, jail, threats of loss of license to all other physicians that showed support or even interest. Is it a surprise that you probably never heard of them before? Or that they were unaware of each other and of their own common roots?

Why the suppression? Shouldn't science be first and foremost interested in truth? When pharmaceutical companies only make money if there is an enemy to be fought, and Pasteur's theory opened the door to this fight. Even today all we hear is 'the war on cancer', 'the war on diabetes'. "He fought hard against the disease" and "I'm going to win this battle against cancer" and so on. The Law of Attraction clearly states what you focus on is all you get. All these 'wars' bring only more of what which they are trying to eradicate. But are they really trying or do they just want us to think so?

At the end of 19th century and into the beginning of 20th, debate was brimming between those who held the monomorphic view and those who held the pleomorphic view of microbes. Unfortunately, Louis Pasteur had more friends in high places than his colleagues and his theory suited the pharmaceutical companies which were on the rise and becoming more and more influential over medical education and research. Antoine Bechamp was largely forgotten, and all who accidentally stumbled onto his theory were persecuted and their careers extinguished.

Towards the end of his life, even Louis Pasteur saw the truth and stated "microbes are nothing terrain is everything". But it was too late. The medical establishment was on a chartered course and it was not going to change.

The entire conventional vaccination philosophy is based on the early theory of Louis Pasteur. This theory is the original quicksand. In order to be objective, conventional medicine still has to prove that a certain microbe caused a certain disease and they have to do it according to Koch's postulates:

1. The microbe must be able to be isolated from the diseased body.
2. The isolated microbe must be cultured outside of the body.
3. When injected into a healthy animal, it must cause that same disease in every case.

You will see that these postulates aren't fulfilled too often. In fact, they're very rarely fulfilled, which raises the question how many vaccines are based on Koch's postulates and how many are useless attempts to chase an imaginary disease?

For more about individual diseases, their symptoms and how to treat them, see my book 'Shots in the Bark'.

VACCINATION FACTS

> "
>
> *"Rabies vaccines are the most common group of biological products identified in adverse event reports received by the USDA's Center for Veterinary Biologics (CVB)."*
> *-World renowned pet vaccination scientist, Dr Jean Dodds*"

The health practice with the second greatest impact (behind nutrition) is today's vaccination protocols. Annual vaccinations are ineffective and dangerous; they wreak havoc upon the cat's natural immune system and, among other issues, are known to cause tumors at vaccination sites. I'd dedicate a whole chapter to this, but I have a book just about this called 'Shots in the Bark'.

The following links will provide you with all the information you need to stand your ground against vaccinations at the vet's office. Annual physicals serve a very important function and protect your cat – annual vaccinations do NOT!

Vaccines Cause Autoimmunity, a conversation between Dr. Lucija Tomljeuovic and Dr. Patricia Jordan, Pet Parents Action Group, June 2012

Why Vets Are Getting Away With Murder, Dana Scott, Dogs Naturally Magazine, March 2012

Feline Vaccine Side Effects, Dr. Michael Lappin, 84th Annual Western Veterinary Conference, February 2012

Vaccines for Cats: We Need to Stop Overvaccinating, Dr. Lisa Pierson, CatInfo.org, July 2011

Don't Vaccinate Your Adult Cat for Distemper, Dr. Jean Hofve, LittleBigCat.com, June 2011

Vaccination, Dr. Jean Hofve, LittleBigCat.com, November 2010

Vets On Vaccines, Dogs Naturally solicits the thoughts of over two dozen holistic veterinarians, April 2012

Dr. Karen Becker discussing the topic with Dr. Ronald Schultz, May 2011:

Part 1: *How Often Should You Vaccinate Your Cat or Dog?*

Part 2: *The Alternative to Re-Vaccinating Your Pets Annually...*

Part 3: *The Vaccine that's Mandatory in EVERY State in America...*

Part 4: *Does Your Pet Really Need That Rabies Shot?*

A Cat's Nine Lives.

Your cat is believed to have nine lives, but these can quickly diminish if you're not careful. The countdown starts even before you bring your kitten home.

Strike one happens in the first two weeks of their life. Many mother cats are either too young or too malnourished to nurse their kittens properly. Some mothers may even get killed or not return, leaving their kittens vulnerable. Kittens need to be with mom for 4 weeks and drink her milk to create their immune systems. If you rescue a kitten at this stage, it will require physical stimulation to poop and warmth as kittens cannot regulate their own body temperatures.

Strike two occurs when you bring your kitten home but neglect to secure it properly. The saying "curiosity killed the cat" is true for a reason—kittens are naturally inquisitive and often wander into dangerous areas, becoming easy prey for dogs, owls, and eagles. You must confine them like a wild animal in an enclosure, providing a litter tray, water, toys, and a feeding plate to keep them safe.

Strike three** happens during a routine vet visit if your kitten is given a deworming medication or, if slightly older, vaccinations. Kittens from birth to two weeks old who haven't developed their immune systems should never be dewormed. Most vets refrain from vaccinating during this period, but succumbing to pressures from over enthusiatic first-time cat parents, some may vaccinate as young as two months old. Even with a minimal dose and the correct deworming agent, these drugs can be toxic. Trials have not tested these medications on kittens, only on adult animals.

There is a significant risk of "sudden death" in kittens, especially in the weaning stage (birth to four weeks old), following the administration of deworming agents. It's crucial to go to the vet for a checkup but refuse deworming. Instead see what resources they can offer you to help you take care of a just born kittens. In cases like this, it is best to find a lactating mom cat who will be happy to feed an extra kitten or two. There are some raw recipes for creating kitten milk replacements online with goats milk, egg yolks and/or beef liver. Do some research.

Strike four is vaccinating your kitten.

Strike five is de-fleaing using anti-flea and tick drugs such as Fipronil.

Strike six is feeding your kitten dry food.

Strike seven is when you try to limit your cat's dry food intake because of budget constraints or because you've heard that too much dry food makes neutered cats obese.

Strike eight is failing to neuter or spay your cat. Cats have a high reproductive drive, and because of their high mortality rates, nature compensates with high birth rates. To ensure a long life for your cat, spaying is essential. Males can be neutered later than females, but females who go into heat will continue doing so until they are spayed. It's virtually impossible, based on my research, to have a long life with a female cat without spaying her.

Strike nine is iatrogenic death—death caused by medical treatment. Every time you take your kitten or cat to the vet, there is a risk. Don't misunderstand; a veterinarian is the first place to go in case of an accident. Veterinary medicine is vital for emergencies and diagnostics, but routine visits can be dangerous for young kittens exposed to deworming medications or vaccinations.

It's essential to use good judgment and take responsibility for your pet, even when consulting a vet.

As your kitten explores new environments, like your home or garden, their immune system is slowly being strengthened. You are naturally immunizing them against environmental factors, but it's crucial not to overwhelm a developing immune system. Gradually introduce your kitten to new people and animals. Initially, a brief outing to your front lawn or garden is sufficient. Avoid unnecessary contact with other cats during the first year. If you must visit the vet, never place your kitten on the floor. Schedule the first appointment of the day, keep your kitten in the carrier, and place them directly on the vet's table. Even though vet clinics and hospitals are regularly cleaned, the cleaning products used can create drug-resistant bacteria and pathogens. Keep your kitten off the ground to minimize exposure.

This book is intended to complement the advice of a veterinarian who can examine your companion cat. While many conditions can be managed with home care, some situations require veterinary assistance. As the animal guardian, you should seek as much information as possible to make informed decisions about your cat's health care. If you have any concerns about your companion cat's safety or health, it is best to get a veterinary examination before attempting home treatment.

Resources And Sources

Dr. Pierson is a California veterinarian, who I was lucky enough to find a year ago when I began sniffing around the whole cat nutrition question; she was featured in an interview with Dr. Karen Becker. The two discuss Dr. Pierson's accumulated wisdom on cat nutrition. I was fascinated with what she shares about how her previous focus on equine medicine informed her understanding of the importance of a species-appropriate diet for felines. If you've not spent time reading and absorbing the great details of hers and other great websites, what are you waiting for?

Important resources for raw feeding for cats:

https://catcentric.org/

Dr Karen Becker DVM- https://www.barkandwhiskers.com/

Lisa A. Pierson, DVM- https://catinfo.org/

Anne Jablonski - https://catnutrition.org/

https://catnutrition.org/faqs/

https://catnutrition.org/recipes/

https://diabeticcatcare.com/

Terri Grow- https://terrigrow.com/blog/

https://tcfeline.com/

Other websites for raw feeding for cats:

https://thelittlecarnivore.com/en/raw-feeding

https://ragdolllove.com/category/cat-nutrition/

https://www.bellaandduke.com/learn/cat-nutrition/raw-feeding-guide-for-cats/

https://rawznaturalpetfood.com/raw-food-diet-cats/

https://barfindia.com/blogs/blog/the-best-way-to-feed-your-cat-raw-food

https://www.rawessentials.co.nz/education/raw-feeding-your-cat
https://tcfeline.com/raw-food-info/
https://felinenutritioncenter.com
https://loveofacat.com/2010/12/the-7-best-natural-commercial-cat-foods-so-far/
https://www.catster.com/nutrition/best-cat-food/
https://www.barkandwhiskers.com/2023-08-01-nl-best-to-worst-pet-food-types/
https://www.claremiddle.com/

Raw feeding calculator:

https://thelittlecarnivore.com/en/blog/calculator-prey-model-raw-plus-diet-for-cats

Books on Nutrition and Raw Feeding

Natural Nutrition for Cats: The Path to Purr-fect Health, 2008, Kymythy R. Schultze, C.N., C.N.C.

Dr Beckers Real Food For Healthy Dogs & Cats - Simple Homemade Food (Karen Shaw Becker Beth Taylor)

Raising Cats Naturally: How to care for your cat the way nature intended, 2003, Michelle T. Bernard

Nutrient Requirements of Dogs and Cats, 2006, National Research Council of the National Academies

Small Animal Clinical Nutrition, 4th Edition, 2000, Mark Morris Institute

Cat Owner's Home Veterinary Handbook, Third Edition, 2008, Debra M. Eldredge, D.V.M, Delbert G. Carlson, D.V.M., Liisa D. Carlson, D.V.M., and James M. Giffin, M.D.

Pottenger's Cats: A Study in Nutrition, 2009, Francis M. Pottenger, Jr., M.D.

Real food for dogs and cats a practical guide to feeding your pet a balanced, natural diet by Middle, Clare Elizabeth

The Raw Meat Cat Food Cookbook - What Your Cat Wants to Eat Whether They Know It or Not by *Holly Ollivander*

Huw Thomas

Books on General Care and Health

The Complete Guide to Holistic Cat Care, 2009, Celeste Yarnall, Ph.D, and Jean Hofve, DVM

Your Cat: Simple New Secrets to a Longer, Stronger Life, 2007, Elizabeth M. Hodgkins, D.V.M., Esq.

Books on Cat Behavior

Cat vs. Cat: Keeping Peace When You Have More Than One Cat, 2004, Pam Johnson-Bennett

Think Like a Cat: How to raise a well-adjusted cat – not a sour puss, 2011, Pam Johnson-Bennett

Naughty No More! 2011, Marilyn Krieger

Books on Animal Welfare and Advocacy

Redemption: The Myth of Pet Overpopulation and the No Kill Revolution in America, 2009, Nathan J. Winograd

Pet Food Industry Practices and Product Safety

Buyer Beware: The crimes, lies and truth about pet food, 2011, Susan Thixton (Ignore the cooking info at the back of the book. Feed raw instead!)

Not Fit for a Dog!: The Truth About Manufactured Dog and Cat Food, 2009, Michael W. Fox, B.Vet.Med, Ph.D, D.Sc., M.R.C.V.S., Elizabeth Hodgkins, D.V.M., and Marion E. Smart, D.V.M., Ph.D.

Sources for information in Chapter #7

Dem Bones...

1. Carlos A. Drisco, et. al, (June, 2007), The Near Eastern Origin of Cat Domestication, Science Express

2. National Research Council (U.S.), (2006), The Nutrient requirements of dogs and cats, National Research Council Ad Hoc Committee on Dog and Cat Nutrition, Chapter One

3. Mark A. Peterson, DVM, (December, 2011), Can Increasing the Amount of Fat or Carbohydrate in a Cat's Diet Compensate for Low Protein Intake?, Insights into

Veterinarian Endocrinology
4. Celest A. Yarnell, Ph.D., (September, 2011), Celestial Homemade Food for Cats, Care2 Make a Difference
5. Feline Nutrition Education Society

Let's Go Shopping!

SHOPPING SOURCES
Here are some places to buy meat online in Bangalore & in metros India

Apps which exclusively sell human-grade meat:
FreshToHome(for Turkey and Quail), Meatigo, Licious, Nandu's, Tendercuts, Netlify
Other Apps: BigBasket, BlinkIt, Zepto
Websites to order meat/organs:
ProteinFresh.In(for buff meat)
Meatright.in
newfrostysonline.com
newkarnatakahamshop.com
RednWhites.com
Raw Food and Freeze Dried Cat Food Suppliers in India:
Frozen ground meatss for your cats: https://barfindia.com/collections/cat-food
Canine India Dehydrated Cat Meal Toppers/Organs: https://canineindia.in/collections/cat-approved
Canine India: Raw Cat & Dog Food
Sourced from local ethical farms in Tamil Nadu and transported in a strict Cold-Chain.
https://canineindia.in/collections/raw
https://caninecraving.com/collections/dog-fresh-meat-seafood
Artico Fresh:
https://www.articofresh.com/product-page/fresh-cat-food-meatychicken
Free Shipping Over Rs.1000
Pawr4Cats | Freeze-Dry Cat Food
Pawr4Cats Rex Series is processed with Freeze-Dry

processing. It dehydrates the meats at sub freezing temperatures keeping it as good as raw. Just add water to make upto 2x the amount of dry food or just feed dry. Can also be used as a topper with your cat food.
https://rawr4dogs.com/pages/pawr4cats
Premium Freeze-Dried Treats
https://alfieandclaire.com/product/premium-freeze-dried-wild-caught-anchovy-treats/
Air Dried treats from Kennel Kitchen. Their wet food is very low in protein so I won't recommend their other products.
https://kennelkitchen.com/collections/cat-food
Ingredients in this are better than whiskas or royal canin since they freeze dry the food. They have their recipe with flax. Someone tell them that Flax is not a bioavaiable source for Omega 3's for cats:
https://goofytails.com/collections/cat-food/products/goofy-tails-wholesome-all-natural-wet-cat-food-and-kitten-food-mackerel-and-seaweed
Journey Raw Dog Food draws on over 13 years of pet industry experience and is dedicated to optimal nutrition and canine health.
https://thepetjourney.in/
Raw Food and Freeze Dried Cat Food Suppliers in US:
https://rawandfresh.com.au/collections/cat-raw-food
7 Best Raw Cat Foods—Healthy Picks for Your Carnivore
https://cats.com/best-raw-cat-food
https://www.amazon.com/raw-cat-food/s?k=raw+cat+food - Pet food companies keep getting sold and bought by bigger conglomerates so always check the ingredients.
https://www.cotswoldraw.com/for-cats
https://www.chewy.com/f/premium-raw-cat-

food_c11741_f3v478370
https://www.lillysadvantage.com/raw-cat-food-products
https://vivarawpets.com/collections/for-cats
https://wefeedraw.com/products
https://www.rawpawspetfood.com/
https://www.freshisbest.com/product-category/cat-food-freeze-dried/
https://primalpetfoods.com/pages/builder?species=cat
https://harc-today.com/

Other Books In This Series

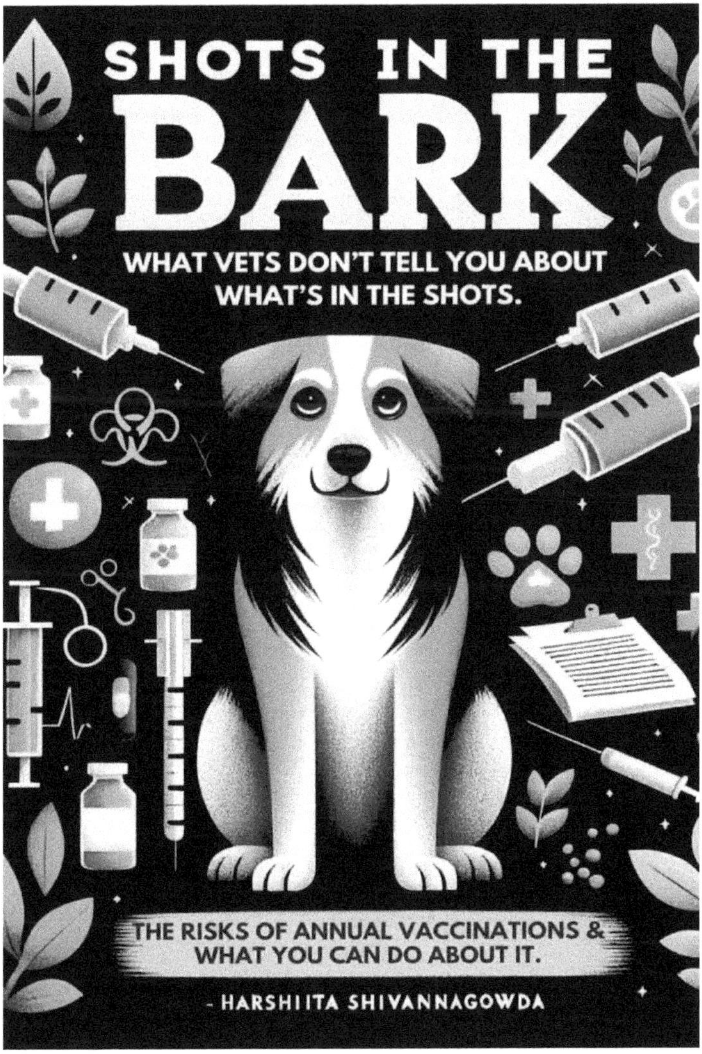

Shots In The Bark(Paperback & Hardcover)

Get in touch:

Instagram: @harsh_truths3321
X:https: x.com/harshtruths3321
Telegram: @harsh_truths3321
Email: harshita.shivanagowda@gmail.com

www.ingramcontent.com/pod-product-compliance
Ingram Content Group UK Ltd.
Pitfield, Milton Keynes, MK11 3LW, UK
UKHW060117010826
14089UKWH00004B/29

9 798895 562437